DATE DUE

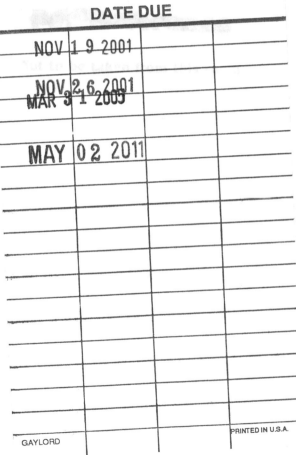

NOV 1 9 2001		
NOV 2 6 2001		
MAR 3 1 2005		
MAY 0 2 2011		

CHARLOTTE'S WEB

A Pig's Salvation

TWAYNE'S MASTERWORK STUDIES

Robert Lecker, General Editor

CHARLOTTE'S WEB

A Pig's Salvation

John Griffith

TWAYNE PUBLISHERS • NEW YORK
Maxwell Macmillan Canada • Toronto
Maxwell Macmillan International • New York Oxford Singapore Sydney

Illustrations Copyright renewed © 1980 by Garth Williams
Selections Reprinted by Permission of HarperCollins Publishers.

Exert from "Lament" by Edna St. Vincent Millay. From Collected Poems,
HarperCollins. Copyright 1921, 1948 by Edna St. Vincent Millay. Used by permission
of Elizabeth Barnett, literary executor.

Twayne's Masterwork Studies No. 12

Charlotte's Web: A Pig's Salvation Context
John Griffith

Twayne Publishers   Maxwell Macmillan Canada, Inc.
Macmillan Publishing Company   1200 Eglinton Avenue East
866 Third Avenue   Suite 200
New York, New York 10022   Don Mills, Ontario M3C 3N1

Library of Congress Cataloging-in-Publication Data

Griffith, John W.
    Charlotte's web: a pig's salvation / John Griffith.
        p.   cm.—(Twayne's masterwork studies; no. 128)
    Includes bibliographical references and index.
    ISBN 0-8057-8812-3 (cloth).—ISBN 0-8057-8813-1 ((ppr)
    1. White, E. B. (Elwyn Brooks), 1899– Charlotte's web. 2. Salvation—In literature.
3. Swine—In literature. I. Title. II. Series.
PS3545.H5187C534   1993   93-35915
813'.52—dc20   CIP

The paper used in this publication meets the minimum requirements of American
National Standard for Information Sciences—Permanence of Paper for Printed Library
Materials. ANSI Z3948–1984. ∞ ™

10 9 8 7 6 5 4 3 2 1 (hc)

10 9 8 7 6 5 4 3 2 1 (pb)

Printed in the United States of America

Contents

Illustrations

E. B. White in 1969.
Courtesy of AP/Wide World Photos

Chronology:
E. B. White's Life and Works

1899   Elwyn Brooks White born on July 11 in Mount Vernon, New York, the youngest of the six children of Samuel Tilly White and Jessie Hart White.

1899–1913   Has (as he remembered it) a happy childhood. All his elementary schooling is at the same school, P.S. 2 in Mount Vernon, where he is a relatively good and diligent student (although he dates his fear of public speaking from these years). At home, learns to play the piano, keeps pets, rides his bicycle, learns a great deal from his brother Stanley, and happily spends a month each summer with his family at Great Pond, a lake in Maine.

1913–1917   Attends Mount Vernon High School, joins a fraternity, assists in editing the school literary magazine, works as a caddy and a surveyor's assistant. In the summer of 1917, serves as a "Farm Cadet" on a farm on Long Island, as a contribution to the war effort.

1917–1921   Attends Cornell University; socializes freely; makes ordinary grades; takes English from William Strunk, Jr., author of the original *The Elements of Style*; writes news, editorials, and light verse for the *Cornell Daily Sun*, of which he becomes editor-in-chief; serves briefly in the Student Army Training Corps in 1918; and graduates in 1921.

1921–1922   Declines the offer of a position teaching English at the University of Minnesota and works briefly for United Press, for a silk mill writing press releases, and for the American Legion News Service.

1922	With his friend Howard Cushman, drives west across the continent, working at odd jobs along the way; writes and sells poems and short prose pieces to various newspapers.
1922–1923	For nine months, works as a reporter for the *Seattle Times;* for three of those months, conducts his own "Personal Column," in which he experiments with brief "items" of the sort he would later perfect with the *New Yorker*. In the summer of 1923, takes a boat trip to Alaska, working for part of his passage.
1923–1925	Returns to New York and begins writing advertising copy, first with the Frank Seaman agency and then with J. H. Newmark; publishes verse and prose in Franklin P. Adams's "The Conning Tower" and other newspaper columns.
1925	On 1 February the first issue of the *New Yorker* appears. Within a few weeks, places his first contribution to the magazine, a spoof on advertising copy.
1926	Takes a boat trip to Europe, earning his way by writing the script for a promotional film for the Cunard Line. Upon his return, goes to work part-time for the *New Yorker*.
1927–1938	His job with the *New Yorker* quickly expands to full-time, and it continues for more than a decade. Writes most of the "Notes and Comment" in "The Talk of the Town" section; writes essays, stories, articles, reviews, and criticism; writes the taglines for newsbreaks and captions for cartoons. Many of his most valued friendships are formed at the *New Yorker*, including those with James Thurber and publisher Harold Ross. Katharine Angell, White's future wife, is a *New Yorker* editor.
1929	Invests money in and helps to operate Camp Otter, where he worked as a counselor several years before. On November 13, marries Katharine Angell. Publishes two books: *The Lady Is Cold*, a book of poetry, and *Is Sex Necessary?, Or Why You Feel the Way You Do*, a spoof of faddish books on sexual psychology, written in collaboration with James Thurber.
1930	On 21 December the Whites' only child, Joel, is born. (Katharine Angell White had two children by her previous marriage.)
1933	The Whites buy the Maine farm that would provide the setting for *Charlotte's Web*.
1934	Publishes a selection of his *New Yorker* paragraphs as a book, *Every Day Is Saturday*. The Whites begin living part time on their Maine farm.

1938   Takes an indefinite leave of absence from the *New Yorker*, and with his family begins living year-round in Maine. Compiles the episodes about a mouse named Stuart Little that he has been writing since the late 1920s and submits them for publication as a book; they are rejected.

1939   Publishes a collection of his satirical pieces from the *New Yorker* as a book titled *Quo Vadimus? Or the Case for the Bicycle*. Signs with *Harper's Magazine* to provide one 2,500-word essay a month, for a column called "One Man's Meat."

1941   Edits with his wife *A Subtreasury of American Humor*.

1942   For the United States Office of Facts and Figures, edits and writes part of a pamphlet on *The Four Freedoms*, a manifesto to be distributed worldwide as part of the Allied war effort; the other contributors are Max Lerner, Malcolm Cowley, and Reinhold Niebuhr. Agrees to make regular contributions to the *New Yorker* (he has never really stopped writing for the magazine). A collection of his "One Man's Meat" essays is published in book form.

1945   As a reporter for the *New Yorker*, and as an enthusiastic advocate of promoting world peace through world government, attends the San Francisco Conference, which would produce the United Nations. Harper's publishes *Stuart Little*, with illustrations by Garth Williams.

1946   Publishes his *New Yorker* articles and editorials on world government as a book, *The Wild Flag*.

1947   The *Atlantic Monthly* publishes his essay "Death of a Pig," about his failed attempt, on his farm, to nurse a pig through erysipelas.

1949   Writes the introduction to a new edition of Don Marquis's *archy and mehitabel*, free verse poems by a literary cockroach about his friend Mehitabel the cat and other talking animals. This project rouses White's interest in writing more talking-animal stories of his own.

1950   Most of the first draft of *Charlotte's Web* is completed.

1952   Publishes *Charlotte's Web*, with Garth Williams's illustrations. It quickly becomes a best seller.

1954   Publishes *The Second Tree from the Corner*, a miscellany of his prose and poetry. At the invitation of the *Yale Review*, writes his fullest tribute to his literary hero Henry David Thoreau, an essay titled "A Slight Sound at Evening."

1959	Revises, edits, and writes a new chapter for *The Elements of Style* by his old Cornell professor William Strunk, Jr. This quickly becomes the most popular English composition handbook of all time.
1960	The National Institute of Arts and Letters awards White its Gold Medal for Essays and Criticism.
1962	Publishes *The Points of My Compass*, a collection of his *New Yorker* essays of the preceding seven years.
1963	President John Kennedy awards White the Presidential Medal of Freedom.
1968–1969	Completes his third children's story, *The Trumpet of the Swan*.
1970	Publishes *The Trumpet of the Swan* with illustrations by Edward Frascino. The Laura Ingalls Wilder Foundation awards White its medal for his contribution to children's literature.
1971	Receives the National Medal for Literature.
1976	*The Letters of E. B. White* are published, edited by Dorothy Lobrano Guth with the assistance of Katharine and E. B. White.
1977	On 20 July Katharine White dies at the age of 85.
1985	On 1 October E. B. White dies at the age of 86.

Note on the Text

For this study, I have used the original hardbound edition of *Charlotte's Web* (New York: Harper and Brothers, 1952), which continues in print. There is also a convenient paperback edition from Dell Publishing Company with different pagination.

1

The Historical Context

E. B. White wrote *Charlotte's Web* during the years 1949–51. It was a time when many Americans were feeling very prosperous, a boom time with high employment, high wages, and high inflation. It was also the first phase of the nuclear age and the cold war, when most of the industrialized world found itself politically aligned with one or the other of two superpowers, the communist Union of Soviet Socialist Republics or the capitalist United States of America. The cold war had gotten hot in Korea, where United Nations forces from the capitalist world had fought to a standoff the armies of communist governments in China and North Korea. In the United States, the mood tended generally to be one of comfort and prosperity, darkened by the real possibility that World War III could break out very suddenly, a war that, it seemed, would leave no survivors.

Is there a dim reflection of the danger of nuclear war in the fact that *Charlotte's Web* centers on a hero who is threatened with a violent death that seems to him arbitrary, pointless, and beyond his control? Possibly there is. Certainly it is true that the children's story White wrote during the 1930s, *Stuart Little*, has no such "apocalyptic" problem at its center, and neither does *The Trumpet of the Swan*

(1970). Does Wilbur's fear of being butchered "symbolize" the fear of hydrogen bombs, ca. 1950? It is possible—though such a correlation is far from obvious, and certainly no part of White's conscious intention. "There is no political meaning in the story" was White's judgment.[1]

In most respects, the relation of *Charlotte's Web* to its historical context is conspicuous by its absence—for what it leaves out rather than what it includes. That is to say, White's story may be historically significant more for its purposeful disengagement from the rigors of the passing scene than for its reflection of them. Knowing what was going on in the world while White was writing *Charlotte's Web* may ultimately be less instructive than recognizing the particular semidetached vantage point that White was privileged to occupy.

Charlotte's Web views life from the perspective of a socially and economically comfortable white male, a man born and raised in a traditional upper-middle-class family that would not have looked out of place in a Norman Rockwell painting. White's father was Samuel Tilly White, an energetic and resourceful man who had left school at the age of 13 and worked his way up to be general manager and a controlling stockholder of Horace Waters & Company, a Brooklyn firm that manufactured pianos. White's mother was Jessie Hart White, whose father had been a successful painter of portraits and landscapes in the middle nineteenth century.

E. B. (the initials stand for Elwyn Brooks) was the youngest of the family's six children. The parents were loving and attentive. Their home was in Mount Vernon, New York, a small, fairly fashionable suburb of New York City. The Whites' house was large and well furnished; it had its own stable, which housed three carriage horses, sometimes a brood of chickens, and occasionally other animals. From his earliest years, White was well supplied with things he enjoyed: bicycles, skates, his own canoe, musical instruments (he became a good pianist), pets of several kinds, and frequent trips into New York City to the Bronx Zoo, circuses at Madison Square Garden, and shows at the Hippodrome. Partly because E. B. suffered from hay fever, the Whites usually spent their Augusts at a camp near a lake in Maine.

White got his college education at Cornell University, where two of his brothers had gone before him. He was there from 1917 until

1921, and he had a good time; he joined a fraternity and a number of other honorary and social organizations, including the Manuscript Club, a group of students and faculty members who met on Saturday nights to discuss their prose and poetry.

World War I brushed White rather lightly. He tried to enlist in 1917, but the army rejected him for being underweight. For five years after he finished college, White wandered around the country and back to New York, working at various jobs in journalism and advertising, selling bits of humorous prose and light verse to an assortment of newspapers. He knew he had a talent for writing, but he was unsure of what to do with it.

Then, in 1925, his destiny found him: journalist Harold Ross brought out the first issue of a sophisticated new weekly magazine called the *New Yorker*, devoted to a witty, satirical, cosmopolitan commentary on life in New York and the rest of the world. Its motto: "Not for the little old lady from Dubuque." Within a few weeks, White had placed his first piece with the magazine, a short bit of satire on advertising. More free-lance pieces from White followed; then, in 1926, White accepted a part-time job with the magazine, editing humorous column-fillers and rewriting items for the featured "Talk of the Town" department.

It would be difficult to overstate the importance, both for White and for the *New Yorker*, of White's affiliation with the magazine. It called for just the sort of journalism White was good at—short, punchy pieces, written with urbanity and humor, playing lightly over the passing scene and not digging too deeply into any of it. For 12 years White ran the "Talk of the Town" and wrote thousands of pieces for the magazine—essays, editorials, short stories, satire, captions, fillers, even advertising. After 1937 he cut back on his work for the magazine, but he continued contributing to it virtually until the end of his life. The majority of everything he had ever published appeared first in the *New Yorker*.

The *New Yorker* was born in the middle of the Roaring Twenties, and it was a child of its age. High-spirited, vaguely irreverent, willing to talk about anything but not to take anything too seriously, its cartoon personification was Eustace Tilley, a dandy in a top hat, cravat, and monocle. White himself was never the gadabout that such an image would suggest; personally, he tended to keep to his quiet ways. But his verbal wit did much to carry the magazine's air of knowing insouciance. Throughout his literary career, at the *New Yorker* and elsewhere, White could afford to stand a certain distance back from the world he wrote about, describing and commenting on it with grace, wit, and humor. He was capable of a certain kind of moral and political seriousness, to be sure, but even that usually had the wry, sportive *New Yorker* tone. His writing is memorable less for the ideas or information it contains than for its style and mood. It tends to omit that which is truly most troubling or intransigent.

In 1933, while much of the Western world was sunk in the Great Depression, White bought a little saltwater farm in Maine, a retreat from the stresses of the New York magazine business. For many years, White spent as much time on the farm as he could, all the while earning his living by his writing. It is this farm that provides the setting for *Charlotte's Web*.

There is no Great Depression on Homer L. Zuckerman's farm in *Charlotte's Web*. There is no war, nor memories of war. There are no politics. There are not even the practical exigencies that make subsistence farming (which seems to be what the Zuckermans are supposed to be doing) a precarious living and a lot of hard work. Fern and Avery Arable have no chores to do. If Mr. Zuckerman feels like supporting a special pig forever, without either breeding or butchering him, he can do it.

Busy as the human and animal characters may be at certain daily routines, life in *Charlotte's Web* is fundamentally life on vacation—vacation from, among other things, history.

2

The Importance of *Charlotte's Web*

Charlotte's Web may be the last of the literary classics for children. Of course, many excellent books for children have been written since *Charlotte's Web* appeared in 1952, and they will undoubtedly continue to be written. Yet it still may be true that *Charlotte's Web* is the last of the classics.

I use the term "classic" here in the sense in which Grimms' fairy tales, *Treasure Island, Alice in Wonderland, Little Women,* and *The Wind in the Willows* are classics, and *The Cricket in Times Square, Roll of Thunder, Hear My Cry,* and *From the Mixed-up Files of Mrs. Basil E. Frankwiler* are not. Classic status in this sense is not simply a matter of literary excellence, but excellence combined with a certain cultural authority, a particular kind of admiration or respect or at least acknowledgment that a book receives, not just among those who know children's literature especially, but among literate people generally. Classics in this sense are stories that large numbers of people have come to think of as being not just good, but indispensable; not just durable, but timeless; not just entertaining or instructive, but somehow definitive.

A classic has, or is perceived by its readers to have, a particularly strong connection with the past: not that it necessarily seems old-fashioned, but that it seems to concern itself with things that have been around a long time. Some stories emerge as classics only gradually. At first, they do not seem to be classics but just good books. Then, as they continue to be read, generation after generation, they come to earn the regard due to old age that has not lost its vitality. Others, and *Charlotte's Web* is among them, seem to have that strong connection with the past from their first appearance.

Paradoxically, there is always something original about a classic, something unique, so that it is not just another example of its genre. The classic does an old thing in a new way, or a new thing in the old way. *Charlotte's Web* is an original hybrid of the old-fashioned realistic story of life on the farm, the talking-animal story, the fairy tale of the innocent saved from death by a magic helper, and a playful satire on gullibility and advertising. Obviously, this is not a "formula" for a classic; as a formula, it is probably a design for disaster. The peculiar components of White's story would fall apart like a house made of straw, were it not for his consummate rhetorical control, his style.

Most readers, child or adult, do not consciously care about style; but they cannot help experiencing it. There is a tranquility about *Charlotte's Web*, a sense of composure, that is largely a function of White's fastidious, restrained, thoughtfully suggestive verbal style. Reading it, one feels the presence of a sensible, careful man—not humorless or unemotional, but a man whose steps are sure and trustworthy because he has taken them with care. Slight understatement is White's credo. The pathos, the humor, the fear, the nostalgic sentiments are all there in the story, felt and conveyed, but almost always with a restraint that comes across as a kind of dignity.

Dignity has a peculiar place in children's literature, since the whole enterprise is often valued specifically because of its freedom from sobriety and self-seriousness. Play, fantasy, magic, nonsense—these are the qualities one associates with children's literature and does not usually associate with dignity. But the classics have dignity.

This dignity or sense of worth occurs in children's literature most often, I think, when one encounters a kind of seriousness beneath the play and the fantasy. As many admirers of sports know, it is quite possible to play games very seriously; and when talented people do it, some kind of greatness is possible. In *Alice in Wonderland*, one perceives the intensity of a hard-edged, logical mind devoting itself rigorously to absurdity; it has the dignity of play performed with great seriousness. In *The Wind in the Willows*, the seriousness is in Kenneth Grahame's uncompromising devotion to the peculiar fantasy of life on the riverbank, his vivid imagination dedicated utterly to the task. Likewise, in *Charlotte's Web*, White plays very seriously. Reading the story, one sees that (a) White is an expert writer, and (b) he respects his story enough to give all his craftsmanship to telling it; therefore, the reader can respect it, too.

Practically speaking, the establishment of a classic in children's literature requires a de facto conspiracy or consensus among three estates: children, parents, and the professional custodians of literature (teachers, librarians, critics, publishers). The three must cooperate to some extent if a book is to be admitted to The Hall of Fame; conversely, each of the three has a sort of veto power. Different classics draw their chief support from different sectors, of course. *The Wizard of Oz* seems to have ridden in mainly on the strength of the children who liked to read it and the other Oz books that followed it. *Alice in Wonderland*, on the other hand, would probably "go out altogether, like a candle" if left entirely to the reading preferences of children. *Alice* is an acquired taste, often acquired long after one's childhood is over. *Alice* needs the support of professional custodians more than, say, *Little Women* does, to maintain its status as a classic.

Charlotte's Web, as far as I can tell, has received abundant approval from all three constituencies. Children seem to enjoy it in a primary way. It is extremely likable from a parental point of view, centering as it does on the wonderfully maternal Charlotte; a parent has grounds for feeling extremely good while reading it aloud at bedtime. The professional custodians are all on White's side; teachers and librarians have admired *Charlotte's Web* from the first, and in recent years it has attracted the attention of literary critics and scholars as well.

Charlotte's Web has particular components and qualities: it tells an ingenious story of a masterful spider who saves a poor pig from death. It confirms old feelings about the American farm as a place of natural decency and harmony. Its subject matter—death, redemption, nature, and the love of animals—is both serious and playful; its tone is both mellow and light. It is a genteel book, civilized and literate. It is highly regarded: millions of readers, both children and parents, are fond of it, and professional people in children's literature have given it the highest marks. These conditions establish *Charlotte's Web* as an immortal children's classic, and it is by no means certain that similar conditions will ever come together in and around one children's book again.

3

The Critical Reception

On its first issuing from Harper's presses in time for the Christmas season in 1952, *Charlotte's Web* moved with almost perfect, unimpeded ease to the heights of popular and critical acclaim. From the time of its initial appearance in the bookstores and book-review columns, there was little doubt that White's story would attract the affection and admiration of almost everyone who read it.

The fact that White was already a well-regarded writer when *Charlotte's Web* appeared (one reviewer referred to him as "*The New Yorker's* beloved E. B. White") and the author of *Stuart Little* (which had sold 100,000 copies in its first year and whose sales were still climbing) assured that his new children's story would receive respectful attention. Most reviewers found that it lived up to and perhaps even surpassed the expectations raised by White's earlier work. Eudora Welty, writing for the *New York Times*, found in it "liveliness and felicity, tenderness and unexpectedness, grace and humor and praise of life, and the good backbone of succinctness that only the most highly imaginative stories seem to grow." She went on: "As a piece of work it is just about perfect, and just about magical in the way it is done."[1]

Pamela Travers, author of the Mary Poppins books, wrote in the *New York Herald Tribune Book Review*: "Every Christmas I find myself playing a sort of literary 'Who's got the slipper?' among the children's books," looking for the book of lasting value. "Twice, and in quick succession, too, the name on the slipper has been E. B. White." She praised *Charlotte's Web* for the "tangible magic" that brings out "the goodness and meaning in simply being alive."[2] *Time* called it "a splendid plum" among a crop of lesser children's stories offered for Christmas-gift buyers that year.[3] The *Atlantic Monthly* referred to it as the second of White's "two perfect books for children."[4] August Derleth, writing in the Madison, Wisconsin, *Capital Times*, said *Charlotte's Web* was "one of those rare stories for young people which bid fair to last longer than their author—a minor classic beyond all question."[5] Not all reviewers were as enthusiastic as these, but almost all of them gave *Charlotte's Web* their solid approval.

Charlotte's Web has been prodigiously popular from the first, and its popularity is durable. In 1984 in his biography of E. B. White, Scott Elledge calculated that more than six million copies of Harper's English editions of *Charlotte's Web* had then been sold. "In its more than twenty translations there is no telling how many copies have been printed."[6] Elledge further points out that *Charlotte's Web* ranked first in a survey that *Publishers Weekly* took in 1976, asking teachers, librarians, publishers, and children's authors to name the 10 best children's books written in America since 1776. Again, in 1987, in a "Reading is Fundamental" survey, *Charlotte's Web* "scored high" among the 750,000 schoolchildren asked to name their favorite book, and it was "overwhelmingly a favorite" among librarians, teachers, and parents who volunteered to help with the survey.[7]

The development of "interpretations" of the story has been rather slight. In his few written remarks on *Charlotte's Web*, White generally tried to discourage ingenious readings. He advised one reader, "When you read it, just relax. Any attempt to find allegorical meanings is bound to end disastrously, for no meanings are in there. I ought to know" (*Letters*, 373). In 1971, in a letter to a director who wanted to adapt *Charlotte's Web* as an animated film, he wrote, "I just want to add that there is no symbolism in *Charlotte's Web*. And there is no political meaning in the story. It is a straight report from the barn cellar, which I dearly love . . ." (*Letters*, 614).

For the most part, writers on *Charlotte's Web* have heeded White's warning. Peter Neumeyer seems to have startled him with a close study of the manuscript versions of the book, which he sent to White and to which White gave this reaction: "Dear Mr. Neumeyer: Thank you for your close reading of *Charlotte's Web*. It is an extraordinary document, any way you look at it, and it makes me realize how lucky I was (when I was writing the book) that I didn't know what in hell was going on. To have known might easily have been catastrophic."[8]

About a dozen scholar-critics have published substantial discussions of *Charlotte's Web* in books and journals. Their work is generally one of two sorts: appreciation of White's literary artistry, or analysis of the thematic content of *Charlotte's Web*.

Neumeyer has published two essays primarily of the appreciative sort. In "What Makes a Good Children's Book? The Texture of *Charlotte's Web*" (1979), he argues for the story's "denseness of texture," saying there "is simply a lot there," generated "by an author with many resources." He finds excellence in White's artistry "ranging from diction to sentence structure, to rhetorical and authorial stance," and places *Charlotte's Web* "in the mainstream of Western literary tradition, drawing for its names, themes, even its plot, from rich classical backgrounds and, insofar as these themselves mirror deepest archetypical truths, drawing on primordial human manifestations." He admires White's simple evocative words that "bespeak their homely Anglo-Saxon origins," his insightful and multilayered humor, and his artfully constructed plot.[9]

The second and more modest of Neumeyer's pieces, "E. B. White: Aspects of Style" (1987), points out certain devices in White's prose: connective repetitions, variation in sentence length, artful mixing of formal and colloquial language, and interesting or surprising juxtapositions.

Roger Sale devotes a long section of his book *Fairy Tales and After: From Snow White to E. B. White* (1978) to *Charlotte's Web*.

Primarily, Sale describes and explains how White created a "hymn to the barn," a celebration of life complete with "the knowledge of transience and death." Sale pays particular attention to the ways in which White moves from his fundamentally realistic first chapters into the mode of talking animals so that "he can show in a nonrealistic way what the life of a barn is really like." He notes how White prepares the way for the understanding that Wilbur and other animals are sentient, sympathetic beings, and how White's characterization of the animals in the story finds a delicate margin that preserves something of their integrity as animals and makes them accessible, and poignant, to human readers. He stresses the numerous lyric passages in the story where White directly praises the beauty of the barn, the seasons and their changing, the songs of the birds and crickets. He calls *Charlotte's Web* "a sweet interlude of a book."

In his essay "Text as Teacher: The Beginning of *Charlotte's Web*" (1985), Perry Nodelman explores in more detail than Sale does the relation between the two opening chapters of *Charlotte's Web*, in which little or no sign is given that Wilbur can think and talk and has a personality, and the rest of the story. Like Sale, Nodelman sees White moving his reader across a bridge from everyday realism to the conventions of the talking-animal story. Nodelman argues, however, that White provides the first two chapters as a means of teaching young readers to read the more imaginatively demanding story that is to follow. He notes that the opening chapters tell the same story, in compressed form, that the Charlotte-and-Wilbur chapters tell: a female of a different species saves a pig from death, makes him her "child" for a time, and is eventually separated from him. Nodelman's thesis is that the opening chapters tell this story "from the viewpoint of innocence," in which events are natural and familiar, dangers are playful or trivial, Fern's wish that the pig be spared is readily granted, and the pig's life as a "baby" is "pure bliss." The central story of Charlotte and Wilbur, Nodelman argues, is more difficult for the young reader, who must now identify with a pig rather than a little girl and must face more of "the troublesome facts of life" than were present when Wilbur lived with Fern. Nodelman says that the Charlotte-and-Wilbur chapters see things "from the viewpoint of experience," which the opening chapters have taught the young reader to "assimilate" or deal with.

Janice M. Alberghene's "Writing in Charlotte's Web" (1985) is primarily of the appreciative sort. Alberghene considers Charlotte's influence on both Fern and Wilbur, and she contends that White's story demonstrates a number of important points about how young and inexperienced users of language can learn from a good model.

Earliest of the expositions of theme in *Charlotte's Web* is Laurence Gagnon, "Webs of Concern: *The Little Prince* and *Charlotte's Web*" (1973). Gagnon applies a concept that he derives from the philosopher Martin Heidegger, the ideal of "living authentically," which he defines as a state of being aware of oneself, being concerned about things and other beings while firmly perceiving one's own difference from them, and coming to terms with the prospect of one's own death. Charlotte, for Gagnon, is a model of authenticity: "From the beginning Charlotte has resolutely advanced toward her own solitary death, all the while taking care of her magnificent web and caring for her humble friend." Gagnon traces Wilbur's progress from a "selfish and insecure" state at the beginning of the story to a state of "authenticity" at the end, a state he achieves by learning to care for Charlotte without losing sight of his difference from her and by his being able to both accept her death and preserve her memory.

My own essay, "*Charlotte's Web*: A Lonely Fantasy of Love" (1980), contends that Wilbur does *not* grow up in any fundamental way. I argue that the heart of White's story is a comforting fantasy in which a scared and vulnerable young creature is briefly confronted by the prospect of loneliness, purposelessness, and his own death, but in the end is spared (primarily through the ministrations of the motherly Charlotte) from having to experience them. I argue that, in this consoling story, Wilbur is blessed with a permanent state of childhood in which he is cared for and protected "all of his days."

Helene Solheim's essay "Magic in the Web: Time, Pigs and E. B. White" (1981) proposes, discursively, to place *Charlotte's Web* in the very center of White's literary vision and work as a whole. She touches on a number of subjects—White's essays "Death of a Pig" and "The Ring of Time," his interest in Thoreau, gender stereotypes in children's fiction. She develops most fully, however, an idea she finds in White: that life is a kind of changing circle, cyclical but mutable in that the individual riders on the turning wheel come and go. She sees images of this perception in Charlotte's web, in the rope swing in the Zuckermans' barn, and in the Ferris wheel at the County Fair.

Norton Kinghorn focuses on the question of "lost innocence" in his essay "The Real Miracle of *Charlotte's Web*" (1986). For him, the "real miracle" is the childlike capacity to converse with animals, appreciate the splendor of nature, and experience "the mystical tie that exists between a sensitive child and the earth and all the creatures and things of the earth." Kinghorn concentrates on Fern's role in the story, and he sees in it a serious "fall from innocence, the loss of paradise." He argues that Fern is important "in the way that Gatsby is important in F. Scott Fitzgerald's *The Great Gatsby*, or that Willie Stark is important in Robert Penn Warren's *All the King's Men*, or Kurtz in Joseph Conrad's *Heart of Darkness*"—that is, as an innocent or well-meaning person who succumbs to the corruption of experience. When Fern wanders off with Henry Fussy at the County Fair and loses interest in Wilbur and Charlotte, Kinghorn describes her as "forever arrested in the world of bright lights, jangling music, the wonderful midway, and the web of the Ferris wheel," a kind of lost soul that has been captured by the "crassly materialist" world of adults from which she never returns. In Kinghorn's description, *Charlotte's Web* comes to sound rather tragic.

Lucy Rollin, in "The Reproduction of Mothering in *Charlotte's Web*" (1990), sees White's story as offering a comforting fantasy in which Wilbur escapes many of the rigors of normal maturity. Using Freudian psychoanalytic principles, Rollin indicates how Wilbur is first mothered by Fern and then by Charlotte, learns or "internalizes" some of the feelings of motherhood for Charlotte's children, but is privileged in the end to live permanently in "an infantile fantasy": "Wilbur's passivity at the end of the book certainly provides a comforting fantasy—especially for a child reader, since it implies that happiness and peace need not be associated solely with maturity and action or with the evolving gender distinctions that seem to accompany maturity. But it also implies the possibility of replicating the mother-child bond without involving a father and suggests that, while the female nurturing characters in the book must grow and change, the chief male one [Wilbur] need not." Rollin praises *Charlotte's Web* for showing that a male can be motherly, thus rising above usual gender stereotypes. She also notes, however, that Wilbur's situation is unusual in the story, where otherwise many of the old male-female distinctions are still clearly in place.

Scott Elledge's indispensable book *E. B. White: A Biography* (1984) contains both appreciation and analysis. Elledge reiterates some things that critics have said about *Charlotte's Web* all along, and he adds some insightful comments of his own. As White's biographer, he calls attention to the story's sources in White's own life, calling it "a fabric of memories" that is "partly, perhaps heavily nostalgic." The nostalgia that he finds in the story is not just personal with E. B. White; *Charlotte's Web* is "a pastoral—an eclogue that takes its readers back to an early vision of an arcadia," the world of the barn, which is a world of lost innocence. Elledge points out that, ecologically, *Charlotte's Web* is "a modern book" with "a humble and skeptical view of the natural world and of the human beings in it," implicitly challenging the chauvinistic notion that people are the only creatures that matter.

4

White's Style

THE *NEW YORKER*

Before he ever wrote a children's story, White perfected his prose style working for the *New Yorker* magazine. From 1926 until 1938, he was primary author of the *New Yorker*'s "Notes and Comment" and other pieces in the editorial section "The Talk of the Town," departments or columns consisting of numerous miniature essays—most of which are one or two paragraphs long—on a wide variety of topics: politics, the change of the seasons, the behavior of celebrities, the pronouncements of bureaucrats and statesmen, nature in the city, automobiles and other odd inventions, the problems of writing, and so on. The predominant mood of this writing was humorous, in accordance with *New Yorker* founder Harold Ross's plan to publish a magazine whose "general tenor will be one of gaiety, wit and satire" (Elledge, 8). Scanning for interesting bits of information in newspapers and magazines, or in his own observations as he went about New York, White would work up, several times each week, a comment containing "a small moral or a few grains of irony," as he once put it (Elledge, 128).

It may seem strange or surprising that a writer who spent most of his literary career writing for a sophisticated magazine like the *New Yorker* should in the end be remembered best for his stories for children. In many respects, however, White's writing for the *New Yorker* was ideal preparation for a children's author. Many of the virtues he cultivated in pieces for "The Talk of the Town" were precisely the qualities that make *Charlotte's Web* the children's masterpiece that it is: brevity, clarity, plain and direct style, simplicity of idea and literary effect, and a pervasive playfulness.

The *New Yorker* format called for complete or self-contained treatment of a topic in a very short space: a few sentences, usually not more than one or two hundred words. The challenge that White had to meet over and over again for 12 years and beyond was to make witty, insightful, or otherwise interesting observations in a few economical strokes. From the first he revealed a unique talent for this kind of writing. Commentators give him credit for more-or-less single-handedly creating the *New Yorker* voice, the *New Yorker* prose style and tone.

Of course, many kinds of writing could *not* be carried out in this special "Talk of the Town" format. One could not tell a long or involved story; one could not provide detailed or complicated information nor work out an extended argument or an idea with several parts to it. A one-paragraph note was not usually an opportunity for White to educate his readers or attempt to change their minds; he had, by necessity, to play rhetorically to attitudes or knowledge that his readers already possessed and to strike quick, definite notes within that range.

WIT, LYRICISM, MORALITY

The note that White struck most often, probably, was the witty or satiric note of irony, underlining the folly or absurdity of something or other with a surprising turn of phrase or a glancing, oblique comparison. One could cite, for example, his comment on a travel brochure he received (in 1935), promising him "the WORLD"—"97 days, $833.50." White's comment: "We had never had the planet laid so neatly at our feet, as though dropped there by a spaniel."[1] Or his item about a Massachusetts poultry farmer who discovered he could soothe his chickens by leaving a radio playing in the henhouse night and day. White's comment: "Somehow it gives us a secret, deep pleasure to know that a dramatized news broadcast, aimed to unnerve the rest of us, is definitely reassuring to a lot of sleepy fowl, dreaming of hawks and weasels in a henhouse far away" (*Writings*, 168). Or his report that, while moving out of his apartment, he was suddenly struck by what a lot of useless possessions he had acquired. "These objects suddenly seemed to be the possessor, ourself the possessed." He completes the paragraph: "An hour later we were wandering dully in the streets seeking lodging in a hotel and passed a little old fellow with all his worldly goods slung on his back in a burlap sack. In his face was written a strange peace" (*Writings*, 199).

The style and tone of pieces like these is pointedly playful: pointed, in that White really does (one assumes) find the travel agency's rhetoric absurd, the newscasters' sense of urgency and importance exaggerated, and his own accumulation of "irrelevant junk" dreary; playful, in that there is an element of pretense or transparent fiction in each of the comments. White does not really envy the homeless man with all his belongings in a burlap sack; he does not really think the chickens' worries about hawks and weasels are interchangeable with what the newscasters have to say; he does not really think that the travel agency has laid the planet at his feet "as though dropped there by a spaniel." The aptness of those propositions, for White's purposes, is in their *limited* literalness. The travel agency is a *little* like a spaniel eagerly offering something to its master; but if the resemblance were more complete and therefore more obvious, it would not be witty. Chicken nightmares and human disasters are, in a sense, balancing but opposed equivalents—the terrors of the one serving as a soporific for the other—but only in a very narrow, particular sense. As for the homeless man with the strange peace written on his face: in another context or in another author (Thoreau, let us say), that comment might be offered in full earnest. In White's piece, however, full of the bad mood of a man who has had to pack up an apartmentful of knick-knacks and appliances, one knows the tongue is in the cheek, the earnestness is deadpan. In order to catch this, one must know—and, in some sense, agree with—White's assumptions. Someone seriously concerned about the plight of the homeless, for instance, might misread White's tone in his reference to the vagrant, or he might disapprove of it—which, in matters of playfulness, is the same as misunderstanding.

White could also achieve a degree of wistful, poetic lyricism in his *New Yorker* pieces. In a paragraph written and published during the Christmas season of 1936, for example, he recalled the Christmas Eve when, as a young man smitten with "calf love," he attended a midnight mass because the girl he loved was to be there. "The snow, the lateness of the hour, the elaborate mysteries of the Mass . . . together with the steady burning vision of the back of Her neck whom we adored, and then the coming out into the snow alone afterward, with the street lamps veiled in white: this indeed was a holy time" (*Writings*, 181). On the death of John F. Kennedy, White wrote that he liked to think of him "without a hat, standing in the wind and weather," exposed to "the cold and wind of these times," in which he "died of exposure." It can be said of Kennedy, wrote White, "that he did not fear the weather, and did not trim his sails, but instead challenged the wind itself, to improve its direction and to cause it to blow more softly and more kindly over the world and its people" (*Writings*, 235). When his friend James Thurber died, White wrote: "During his happiest years, Thurber did not write the way a surgeon operates, he wrote the way a child skips rope, the way a mouse waltzes" (*Writings*, 234).

The playful note is audible even in such expressions of sentiment; there is a smile in White's tone when he thinks of his young self having "a steady burning vision of the back of Her neck whom we adored," or Thurber writing his pieces "the way a mouse waltzes." The effect—even when humor is subsumed in warmer sentiments—is related to his satiric touches. It, too, depends on suggesting a resemblance between things alike in only certain ways: Kennedy's assassination like dying of exposure "to the cold and wind of these times," Thurber's writing like a child skipping rope or a mouse waltzing, the love-struck boy having a "holy" experience as he invades a cathedral to peek at his girl. Here as with the satire, one must assume White's assumptions without instruction from him; and understand that a waltzing mouse is charming and magical, not freakish or grotesque; and that innocent young love (notice, the boy comes out of the church "alone"; he is not "making a move") is no sacrilege in a place of worship; and that calling Kennedy's a death from exposure is meant as a tribute. The style is, in its modest way, sophisticated, in that it is knowing rather than instructive; it assumes the reader's agreement rather than arguing for it.

White's style does involve *evaluation* all along, of course—moral, aesthetic, or commonsensical: advertising rhetoric is ridiculously ingratiating, possessions are a snare for the spirit, Kennedy was a dashingly courageous man; but the evaluation is implicit, not explained. Sometimes White's pieces would come closer to making his judgment explicit and find what he called "a small moral" in his subject. What this meant, in practice, is that sometimes he would take up subjects about which he could not be quite so confident that his readers shared his feelings—and then his evaluative nudging had to be a little stronger. For example: in the years following World War II, White particularly espoused the idea of a world government as the only effective means of preventing future wars. He devoutly supported the United Nations as a step in the right direction. In a brief, 85-word "Comment" in 1946, he noted a sign on a New York City street corner pointing the way to UN Headquarters. "The arrow is vertical," he wrote, and this is the "conventional highway 'straight ahead' indication." But for him, "far gone in meditation," the arrow "distinctly pointed straight up past the dingy railroad tracks and on into Heaven" (*Writings*, 84). End of piece. When the Apollo 11 mission landed on the moon in 1969, and Neil Armstrong and Buzz Aldrin planted an American flag there, White noted the fact with a shake of his head. "What a pity that in our moment of triumph we did not forswear the familiar Iwo Jima scene and plant instead a device acceptable to all: a limp white handkerchief, perhaps, a symbol of the common cold, which, like the moon, affects us all, unites us all" (*Writings*, 102).

Even here, where the idea of unifying humanity is quite sober, White retains the light and playful spirit: a street sign pointing to

Heaven, a limp handkerchief as the emblem of universal humanity. To be witty in White's way is always to risk seeming not quite sincere or not quite serious or not quite rigorous; sometimes White has been criticized for a lightness not only of spirit but of mind. "The *New Yorker* has always dealt with experience not by trying to understand it but by prescribing the attitude to be adopted toward it," said one reviewer of *Wild Flag*, White's book on world government. "This makes it possible to feel intelligent without thinking, and it is a way of making everything tolerable, for the assumption of a suitable attitude toward experience can give one the illusion of having dealt with it adequately."[2] In an otherwise laudatory review of a book of White's *Harper's* pieces, Diana Trilling wrote that "in the matter of style, real as his gifts are, we question whether his felicity has not sometimes been achieved by going around rather than over intellectual hurdles."[3] White, over the years, had to get used to this kind of criticism. "The world likes humor, but it treats it patronizingly," he wrote. "It feels that if a thing is funny it can be presumed to be something less than great, because if it were truly great it would be wholly serious."[4]

THE NOT-QUITE-PLAIN-STYLE

However one ultimately appraises White's moral or intellectual stature, the fact remains that he did develop in his *New Yorker* pieces a style that was serviceable for many purposes. It was both artless and quite artful. Its artlessness, its apparent ease and naturalness, consists primarily of the fact that White customarily worked with general, uncomplicated ideas, used relatively simple and familiar words (one seldom needs a dictionary in reading White), and cast his mostly short, declarative sentences in syntax that was crisp, definite, and precise. Brevity and clarity were his avowed objectives; he often advised young writers just to say what they meant, in the fewest, most concrete, and active words possible.

Peter Neumeyer, in his essay "E. B. White: Aspects of Style," points out one mannerism that gives White's style some of its distinctive flavor: White generally establishes a norm of written Standard

English—the formal, correct idiom of educated writers—and then occasionally "breaks style" by "dipping into the colloquial" and using expressions like "what in hell was going on" or "in a class by itself." It is also true, though, that (in his *New Yorker* writing at least) White also makes the opposite maneuver. Even though one of his tips to writers in *The Elements of Style* was to "avoid fancy words" ("Anglo-Saxon is a livelier tongue than Latin, so use Anglo-Saxon words."), in his own practice he achieved a certain sportive tone by occasionally flirting with poeticism or "fine writing." At crucial moments he can refer to "the lovely arabesques of the Jersey shore" (*Writings*, 118), to tadpoles as "gloomily metamorphic" (*Writings*, 150), or to "the disinclination of all things, animate or inanimate, to let go of life" (*Writings*, 178).

Like his phrasing, White's way with syntax plays off just slightly against the norms of middle-range Standard Written English. Sometimes he will indulge in a conspicuous dramatic parallelism, as when he ends a "Notes and Comment" piece on the collection of scrap metal for use in the war: "Scrap iron, scrap steel, scrap gold. Scrap life" (*Writings*, 80). Or he might risk a heavily periodic climax: "The snow, the lateness of the hour, the elaborate mysteries of the Mass . . ., together with the steady burning vision of the back of Her neck whom we adored, and then the coming out into the snow alone afterward, with the street lamps veiled in white: this indeed was a holy time." Such conspicuous structures as these notify the reader that White is not just saying the first thing that occurs to him in the easiest way possible; they signal that a craftsman is at work, so that even when the structures are simple, they are not careless.

Generally, White's prose is not showy, but steadily obedient to the sensible rules for clarity and correctness that he advanced in *The Elements of Style*: "Keep related words together." "Express coordinate ideas in similar form." "Place the emphatic words of a sentence at the end." "Make the paragraph the unit of composition." "Prefer the standard to the offbeat." Mechanically—that is, in grammar and syntax—White seldom aspires to much more than grace and correctness. Correctness provides the white screen on which the muted colors of his emotional tone can play.

White once told an interviewer, "I don't care about being known as a writer. I just want to be thought of as a reliable man" (Elledge, 220). In several respects, the figure that emerges in White's prose is just that: a reliable man writing: steady, unpretentious, meticulous, given to only milder flights of playfulness and satire, but never to nonsense; inclined toward nostalgia and other wistful sentiments at times, but usually with some gesture that indicates he knows he is indulging himself.

This persona and this style, which White developed in his *New Yorker* work, is (with only slight modification) the persona and the style of the White who narrates *Charlotte's Web*.

NEW YORKER STYLE AND CHARLOTTE'S WEB

In particular, White's habit of composing in short, self-contained units is evident in *Charlotte's Web*. *Stuart Little* is more obviously episodic in structure than is *Charlotte's Web*, but it is nonetheless true that *Charlotte's Web* divides readily into brief set pieces or discrete compositional units of a few hundred words apiece: Fern's acquiring Wilbur from her father; her devotion to Wilbur as a make-believe baby; the broadly comic account of Wilbur's escape from the pigpen, and of his attempt to spin a web; Charlotte's stories about her cousin; Mrs. Arable's visit to Dr. Dorian; and so on. Some sections of the book, especially extended passages of description, could, with just the addition of a rhetorical flourish at the end, pass for one of White's more poetic or sentimental *New Yorker* notes: the two-paragraph description of the barn at the beginning of chapter 3; the five-paragraph description of early summer days at the beginning of chapter 5; Charlotte's meditation on the folly of human "web-spinning" in chapter 9; the long paragraph about rope-swinging in the barn in chapter 10 (finished off with White's remark about parents' groundless fears that children will fall and hurt themselves); the description of the crowd that gathers to witness the "miraculous" web in chapter 11; the description of the coming of autumn and winter in chapter 22. In each of these instances, White interrupts whatever larger narrative momentum he has built up to contemplate ("Notes and Comment" style) a place, a time of year, a children's game.

This kind of interruption might be inappropriate in another sort of story; but *Charlotte's Web* conspicuously avoids the kind of progressive development of plot or situation that such interludes might damage. Consider the fundamental plot-generating predicament, and how White handles it: Zuckerman is raising Wilbur to butcher him. This threat of death is a prospect that another writer might have played for apprehension or suspense. But White, after announcing the bad news that Wilbur is to be killed, and introducing Charlotte, who promises that she will not permit that to happen, pushes the menace of butchery into the background. He never shows the Zuckermans deliberating on whether to butcher Wilbur or not, and he never establishes, in advance of their being achieved, the conditions crucial to Wilbur's salvation. The illusion of possible defeat arises briefly at the County Fair when a big stupid pig called Uncle wins the blue ribbon, and Templeton speculates that Zuckerman may decide to butcher Wilbur after all. But that is just Templeton talking. Wilbur's special excellence all along has been associated with a kind of blessing from above, the miracle of the web that prompts Lurvy to say a prayer and the minister to preach a sermon about being "on the watch for the coming of wonders."

5

Why a Pig Should Be Saved

CHARACTER

White's handling of character permits him the maximum latitude for interludes and self-contained set pieces. *Charlotte's Web* is not a story of growing or changing personalities, the curve of which must be kept clearly in view. This may seem a surprising statement, in view of the fact that a prominent theme or idea in the story is Fern's going through a sequence of phases. But this supposed exception to the principle most clearly shows its validity: Fern does not steadily grow or change in the story. White shows her in three distinct phases, but he forgoes any dramatization or explanation for how or why she moves from one phase to the next. In chapters 1 and 2, she is a little girl who loves to pretend her little pig is her doll or her baby; Wilbur is an animal on which she can project her fantasies. In chapters 3 through 14, she is purely a passive, quiescent observer, watching and listening to the barnyard animals attentively, projecting no fantasies, taking no active part, not even protesting when she hears (with the animals) that Wilbur is to be killed. Chapter 14 concerns Mrs. Arable's visit to Dr. Dorian, and his assuring her that there is nothing wrong with Fern's spending time "alone" in the barn. From that point on, Fern, to all intents and purposes, disappears from the barn. With the coming of autumn, her return to school, and the trip to the County Fair, Fern is abruptly in phase three, her new friendship with Henry Fussy and virtual indifference to Wilbur. When Wilbur is awarded his special prize, Fern chooses to be somewhere else, riding the Ferris wheel with Henry Fussy.

Fern changes, but the changes are simple and sudden, and they require no steady concentration on what is going on with her. The other characters in the story do not change at all. From the first time he speaks, Wilbur is the wistful child, seeking protection, care, and companionship. At the end of the story he is the same child, now assured of protection, care, and companionship. Charlotte is, of course, Charlotte; she appears in the barn, fully formed and omnicompetent, and requires no change. Templeton is the irascible self-seeker when first he speaks ("I prefer to spend my time eating, gnawing, spying, and hiding. I am a glutton but not a merry-maker" [29–30]), and the same when he speaks his final line ("I am naturally a heavy eater and I get untold satisfaction from the pleasures of the feast" [175]). Fern's brother Avery, from his first introduction, "heavily armed," in chapter 1, is the rowdy American boy every time he comes into the story. Conceiving his characters as he does, fully set and defined from the outset, White is free to concentrate, chapter by chapter and paragraph by paragraph, on immediate, local descriptions, exchanges of dialogue, and comic or dramatic turns. Seldom does White appear to push his characters in directions that the plot or a theory of personality development might require them to go.

Several times in his story, for example, White indulges in a comic turn that depends on the reader's relative unconcern with character development or even character revelation. This is the humor he derives from having a character speak in terms that are comically formal, or pointedly too elevated for the situation. Charlotte does this frequently: she recites the zoologist's Latin names for the eight sections of her legs, for example (55); or she says "Salutations" instead of "Hello," and then explains that "'salutations' . . . is just my fancy way of saying hello or good morning" (35). An overlay of pedantry is a consistent trait of Charlotte's character, indulged in primarily for humor's sake. But White will occasionally have his other characters philosophize in ways that are strangely and humorously out of key with their situations. For instance, in chapter 4, "Loneliness," Wilbur asks a lamb to play with him, and the lamb rudely replies, "Pigs mean less than nothing to me." In reply, Wilbur launches into a disquisition on "nothingness." "What do you mean, *less* than nothing? I don't think there is any such thing as *less* than nothing. Nothing is absolutely the limit of nothingness." He persists: "It's the lowest you can go. It's the end of the line. If there were something that was less than nothing, then nothing would not be nothing, it would be something—even though it's just a very little bit of something." He rests his case: "But if nothing is *nothing*, then nothing has nothing that is less than *it* is" (28).

This purports to be the speech of a two-month old piglet, trying to make friends with a lamb. No one knows how such a creature would "really" talk; yet it is clear that White's humor here derives from the charming absurdity of Wilbur's talking this way, so logically and even philosophically.

Templeton has comparable moments of comic verbosity. For instance, when he agrees to go to the County Fair with Wilbur and Charlotte, he worries about Wilbur's stepping on him while he is hiding in Wilbur's crate. "'Struggle if you must,' said he, 'but kindly remember that I'm hiding down here in this crate and I don't want to be stepped on, or kicked in the face, or pummeled, or crushed in any way, or squashed, or buffeted about, or bruised, or lacerated, or scarred, or biffed'" (125). A rat warning a pig not to step on him, Templeton sounds like a lawyer trying to close the loopholes in a contract.

The announcer at the County Fair, introducing Wilbur for his Special Prize, provides another example of White's humor of overformality: "Many of you will recall that never-to-be-forgotten day last summer when the writing appeared mysteriously on the spider's web in Mr. Zuckerman's barn, calling the attention of all and sundry to the fact that this pig was completely out of the ordinary." Public-address announcers are entitled to a certain degree of stilted formality; but theological speculation? "This miracle has never been fully explained, although learned men have visited the Zuckerman pigpen to study and observe the phenomenon. In the last analysis, we simply know that we are dealing with supernatural forces here, and we should all feel proud and grateful" (157).

The central concept of the words in Charlotte's web and their effect on the people who see them is, in itself, a satiric idea with ties to White's career at the *New Yorker*: White's story contains at its core a good-natured parody of an advertising campaign. For two years before he went to work for the *New Yorker*, White worked for a New York advertising firm. When he moved on to the magazine, he wrote a number of satiric pieces on advertising, including some advertisements for the *New Yorker* itself that parodied the improvement-through-culture ads that were popular in the 1920s. Charlotte's scheme for saving Wilbur is the same scheme by which advertising people make their livings: when people are impressed by honorific words written about some product in an unusual, eye-catching medium, they may attribute the impressiveness to the product (Wilbur) rather than to the ingenuity of the copywriter (Charlotte), where it belongs. It is gullibility that makes advertising work, and it is gullibility that saves Wilbur's life. People are gullible, thinks Charlotte. "If I can fool a bug, I can surely fool a man. People are not as smart as bugs" (67). When the words begin appearing in the web, it crosses Mrs. Zuckerman's mind that the spider, not the pig, is unusual. But her point gets lost in the ensuing uproar.

This and other "grains of irony" of the sort White sought for his *New Yorker* pieces are scattered all through *Charlotte's Web*. But the dominant tone of White's story is not satiric; it is nostalgic.

NOSTALGIA AND CHILDHOOD

Authors who have made careers of writing in other genres often grow nostalgic when they turn to writing for children, and understandably so. In *Charlotte's Web*, White looked back fondly and with a glow of sentiment on the charm of childhood. Scott Elledge calls the story "a fabric of memories, many reaching back much further in time than

White's life on his farm. It is a pastoral fiction written when, more than ever before, White's vision was retrospective and his sense of life was sharpened by his having seen many things come to an end" (300). In some minor respects the story draws on White's own boyhood experiences: Fern's interest in animals reflects White's own similar interest as a child, and his loving recapitulation of the things and atmosphere of life in the barn has roots in the memories of his own earliest years. More important, though, nostalgia operates in *Charlotte's Web* in the tone and attitude White takes toward childhood itself.

There are actually two versions of childhood in *Charlotte's Web*—one dramatized in the story of Wilbur, the other in the story of Fern, both of them stylized conceptions of the child-state. It is with Fern that White can write most freely in the nostalgic mode, since she is relatively tangential to the central plot and so is available for acting out certain notions of "how kids are." The childlike qualities that White emphasizes in Fern are her sympathy with cute little animals, and animals that are not so cute, like spiders and rats; her enjoyment of simple activities like playing with dolls, swinging on a rope swing in the barn, and riding the Ferris wheel with Henry Fussy; and her serene and dreamy nature. Ultimately, she is the child as natural, un-self-conscious, receptive innocent; the child as appreciator, as unfocused, relatively ego-free learner.

To some extent, Fern's easygoing nature is a function of the fact that her character was added late, after the story of Wilbur and Charlotte had been written; her involvement in the central plot of "a pig shall be saved" and the web-writing is intermittent and peripheral. After the opening chapters, in which Fern flares up passionately to save Wilbur's life and then devotes herself to him as a make-believe baby, she becomes purely an observer. The day that Wilbur learns of the "conspiracy" to butcher him, with Fern looking on and listening all the while, she does not even mention it to her family when she reports what is going on in the barn. A strategic reason why White has her make no effort to intervene in this second threat to Wilbur's life is that White knows that Charlotte, not Fern, is to be the savior this time, and to have Fern carrying on as she did in chapter 1 would make it harder for Charlotte to effect her subtler and more oblique solution. But Fern's surprising silence on this newest danger to Wilbur ultimately fits in with White's idea of the kind of child she is. Her detachment here will later to turn to positive indifference to Wilbur's fate, when she goes off to ride the Ferris wheel with Henry Fussy rather than watch Wilbur receive his special medal at the County Fair.

Midway through the story, Dr. Dorian makes an observation on E. B. White's behalf: "Children pay better attention than grownups" (110). This, in the context of *Charlotte's Web*, is true. But there is a corollary: children have short attention spans. Their passions and concerns are relatively superficial and transitory. In the course of a few months, Fern moves from ardent devotion to Wilbur as "her baby," to a reflective interest in his fortunes in the barn, to a new and supplanting ardor for Henry Fussy and Ferris wheels. White assigns no moral discredit to Fern's fickleness in the story; on the contrary, it is part of the charm of childhood. Fern moves from one phase to the next as naturally and appropriately as the baby spiders spin their balloons and fly away. This is perhaps White's most nostalgic axiom: children are blessedly free to follow their whims and fancies where they lead. Fern's defection from Wilbur's cause does no damage; it is harmless, a positive manifestation of her childlike freedom.

Much of *Charlotte's Web* is told, not from Fern's point of view, but from a "Fern-like" point of view, a patient, attentive, receptive, unjudgmental appreciation of little things. As Fern might do, White lingers over the sights and sounds and smells of the barn and his other settings. Eight or nine times in *Charlotte's Web* White stops his narrative completely just to catalog homely details: the tools and other equipment in the Zuckermans' barn; the specific components of the slop in Wilbur's trough; the steps in cutting hay with horse-drawn mowing machines; the songs of several specific birds in early summer; the things a child can see if she looks closely at the dandelions and clover and potato vines; the 11 different makes of cars and trucks that arrive at the barn when Wilbur becomes famous; the contents of the Zuckermans' dump; the "veritable treasure" of edible leftovers a rat can find at the County Fair late at night; and the particular changes in the woods and the weather when the seasons change.

These items go to make up "the glory of everything" in White's story—not because most of them are particularly glorious or striking or even especially interesting in themselves, but because they are part of a treasured past whose pastness enhances their value. *Charlotte's Web* contains a few hints that White, writing in 1950, really pictured events taking place in the days of his own youth. For example, the farmers pull their mowers with horses and Fern carries a bucket of hot water up to her room when she wants to bathe. Virtually everything in the story could have happened in 1910, when White was a boy, as easily as in 1950, when he wrote it. It would change the whole mood of the story to introduce, for example, a television set, or even a radio, into the Arable living room. But whether the machines are old-fashioned or newfangled does not really matter very much. Whatever year it is when Charlotte introduces letters into spiderwebs, the pleasure White brings to the homely details is the feeding of nostalgic appetites. His fond catalogs of all the things that busy grown-ups pay no attention to are attractive because they invite readers to imagine how nice it would be (or, if they take White's reconstruction of childhood literally, how nice it actually was) to have the time and untroubled spirit to dwell on them.

CHILDHOOD AS ORDEAL

It is not easy to reconcile perfectly White's other version of childhood—Wilbur, the pig—into this idyllic and nostalgic atmosphere, but it does ultimately fit. Obviously Wilbur is, on some level, a child. White has imagined him with a child's personality: his desire for playmates, his reluctance to go to sleep at bedtime, his delight in hearing stories and lullabies, his curiosity about words and odd facts, and his susceptibility to boredom and anxiety are all features having more to do with human children than with young pigs. Whatever his personality, though, the "facts" are that Wilbur lives locked up in a barn and is being raised and fattened for the butcher. A pig—not a child—shall be saved; and no simple reading of *Charlotte's Web* is likely to raise thoughts in most readers' minds that Wilbur's situation—as a creature threatened with butchery—is paradigmatic of childhood.

Many things can happen, though, when a writer projects a human personality on an animal—some of them under the author's control, some perhaps not; some advantageous to the author's conscious purposes, some perhaps subversive to them. Crucial to the drama of *Charlotte's Web* is the notion that Wilbur is aware of himself as a self and can contemplate, with considerable understanding, his own impending death. This is crucial not just to the sense of crisis in the story, but to White's implicit argument for why Wilbur should be saved: to kill Wilbur would be, de facto, to kill a person. For readers who think about it, Wilbur's realization of the prospect of death has to be seen as a human rather than a porcine ordeal. Though it is his situation as a pig that produces the trauma, Wilbur experiences it as a child's first awareness that some day he must die. For Wilbur, life is— or threatens to be—a condition of fear, helplessness, boredom, and loneliness. Thanks to Charlotte and the plot of the story, all these woes will be overcome. Still, could it ever be accurate to say that a children's story focusing on such a melancholy condition is inherently nostalgic?

Actually, it could be—and, in the case of E. B. White, probably is. White could on occasion claim a nostalgic feeling even for the pains of one's earlier years: "A man sometimes gets homesick for the loneliness that he has at one time or another experienced in his life and that is a part of all life in some degree," wrote White. He said that "a secluded and half-mournful yet beautiful place will suddenly revive the sensation of pain and melancholy and unfulfillment that are associated with that loneliness, and will make him want to seize and recapture it." He called the feeling a "passing want," not a chronic condition; but he did testify to having it.[1] Perhaps the experience of being "homesick" for "loneliness . . . pain and melancholy and unfulfillment" is peculiar to White and a small fraction of the human race; perhaps it is a common feeling. Whichever the case, it does seem fair to say that, in White's emotional economy at least, the nostalgic mood of *Charlotte's*

Web can encompass the wistful contemplation of the ordeals of childhood as well as the pleasures.

In 1940, several years before he wrote *Charlotte's Web*, White wrote an essay on freedom that is one of the most soberly philosophical things he ever produced. In thinking about freedom, White found himself thinking about selfhood, and the process whereby one comes to think of oneself as an individual. The process began, he wrote, with a child's "haunting intimation (which I presume every child receives) of his mystical inner life; of God in man; of nature publishing herself through the 'I.'" He identified this haunting, mystical insight with certain kinds of childhood experiences: "a boy, we'll say, sitting on the front steps on a summer night, thinking of nothing in particular, suddenly hearing as with a new perception and as though for the first time the pulsing sound of crickets." At that moment the boy is struck "with the novel sense of identification with the natural company of insects and grass and night, conscious of a faint answering cry to the universal perplexing question, 'What is "I"?'" He offers another example of such a moment—a glimpse of death: "a little girl, returning from the grave of a pet bird, leaning with her elbows on the windowsill, inhaling the unfamiliar draught of death, suddenly seeing herself as part of the complete story." His third instance of the self-awakening moment is "an older youth, encountering for the first time a great teacher who by some chance word or mood awakens something and the youth beginning to breathe as an individual and conscious of strength in his vitals" (*OMM*, 208–10).

White's subject here is the awakening of the sense of the individual self, the essential "I" for whom freedom is such a precious condition. Dim outlines of *Charlotte's Web* are visible in his three examples of children experiencing this awakening: the boy "sitting on the front steps on a summer night, thinking of nothing in particular, suddenly hearing as with a new perception and as though for the first time the pulsing sound of crickets" could, with a little adjustment, be Fern. The youth "encountering for the first time a great teacher" could be Wilbur listening to Charlotte. And the little girl whose bird has died, "inhaling the unfamiliar draught of death," could be Wilbur as he realizes his own death's possibility.

In the essay on freedom, White draws these three "typical" moments together as instances of a child's first insight into his or her place in the universe, a "faint" answer to "the universal perplexing question: 'What is "I"?'" White assigns no such explicit meaning to their counterparts in *Charlotte's Web*. In the essay, he philosophizes; in the story, he does not. But in both cases he draws on his sense of what it is, or what it means, to be a child. In both cases his imagination gravitates toward similar brushes with nature, death, and a wise older figure. Though the experiences themselves are somber, White's attitude toward them, in both the essay and the story, is nostalgic.

Reviewing *Charlotte's Web*, Pamela Travers wrote: "In spite of all the comedy, it has an absorbed and dreamlike air such as one sometimes surprises in a child playing alone."[2] The "absorbed and dreamlike air" and the comedy are not, however, basically contradictory. *Charlotte's Web* is an extension of the *New Yorker*'s "Notes and Comment" formula into a full-length children's story. White's *New Yorker* notes were a kind of meditation: brief exercises in focusing on some odd or touching or otherwise suggestive fact or incident, and sketching it in such a way as to bring out "a small moral or a few grains of irony." Like those pieces, *Charlotte's Web* is playfully meditative. The "small morals" are there—the value of friendship, the wisdom or rightness of nature, the blessing of childhood. The "grains of irony" are there, too—dissolved and diffused somewhat, but giving nonetheless the playful spirit, the stylistic twinkle in the eye that was E. B. White's most consistent trademark.

THE BUTCHER FOILED

Charlotte's Web began not as a tribute to friendship but as a story about saving a pig's life. White described its genesis in a letter to Bennett Cerf for his "Trade Winds" column in the *Saturday Review of Literature*, at the time *Charlotte's Web* was published. "I have been asked how I came to write 'Charlotte's Web,'" White wrote. "Well, I like animals, and it would be odd if I failed to write about them. Animals are a weakness with me, and when I got a place in the country I was quite sure animals would appear, and they did."[3]

As a lover and keeper of animals, though, White was bothered by the usual destiny of animals on a farm. "A farm is a peculiar problem for a man who likes animals because the fate of most livestock is that they are murdered by their benefactors. The creatures may live serenely but they end violently, and the odor of doom hangs about them always." White noted that he himself had kept several pigs, "starting them in spring as weanlings and carrying trays to them all through the summer and fall. The relationship bothered me." He would become acquainted with his pig, "and he with me, and the fact that the whole adventure pointed toward an eventual piece of double-dealing on my part lent an eerie quality to the thing" (Trade Winds, 6).

White felt that keeping and forming an acquaintanceship with a pig that he would then kill was a form of treachery. "I do not like to betray a person or a creature, and I tend to agree with Mr. E. M. Forster that in these times the duty of a man, above all else, is to be reliable." It became troublingly clear to him, White wrote, that "as far as the pig was concerned I could not be counted on." And his mind turned to the situation that would become *Charlotte's Web*. The theme of his story, White wrote, "is that a pig shall be saved, and I have an idea that deep inside me there was a wish to that effect" (Trade Winds, 6).

A pig should be saved; that was primary. The next question was, How? As White wrote in a letter to an admirer: "I had made up my mind to write a children's book about animals, and I needed a way to save a pig's life, and I had been watching a large spider in the backhouse, and what with one thing and another, the idea came to me" (*Letters*, 375). The title of the story is not "Charlotte and Wilbur" or "A Peculiar Couple" or anything referring to their relationship, but rather, as it should be, "Charlotte's *Web*." Charlotte's lifesaving device of writing in the web is the imaginative center of the story; matters of social and personal connections surrounding it are, in an important sense, secondary.

From the outset, Charlotte's interest in Wilbur is explicitly and directly tied to the idea "a pig shall be saved." She befriends Wilbur because he needs help, because he is lonely and in danger, because he is pitiful. From that beginning, White suggests, grows a bond that can suitably be called friendship. But by comparison with other friendships in literature or in life, it is a very peculiar one. It is a friendship devoted to taking care of Wilbur; the only substantial interests that Charlotte and Wilbur share are those directly related to Wilbur's well-being. Charlotte is to Wilbur as a social worker might be to the inmate of a prison, as a foster mother is to an abandoned child, and as a schoolteacher is to a very young and anxious pupil. She is older and wiser than Wilbur; she is resourceful and self-reliant while he is helpless and dependent; she is generous and self-sacrificing while he is gratefully receptive. Affection is mutual between them, but in every other respect their friendship is all give on Charlotte's side, all take on Wilbur's. This, of course, is in line with the kernel idea of the story, that a pig shall be saved.

Charlotte and Wilbur never play together; they never argue or compete; they never join in any enterprise on any sort of equal terms; they are never peers. In fact, the more ordinary kind of friendship does not seem to be either a dream or a possibility for Wilbur. (This apparently bothered the makers of the animated cartoon film version of *Charlotte's Web*. With no authority from the novel, they provided Wilbur with a gosling friend who is more his equal.) In concluding his story, White proclaims that Wilbur's need for friends is permanently filled; as each new generation of spiders appears, while a few volunteer to stay in the barnyard and keep Wilbur company, the rest fly away. This, the story implies, is satisfactory. (In a limited way, this ending echoes the conclusion of *Peter Pan*, where motherly girls continue to appear in generation after generation, and Peter is content with whichever girl happens to be on hand when he needs one.)

CROWDS AND LONERS

In *Charlotte's Web*, ordinary or natural communities do exist; sheep are friends with sheep, geese are friends with geese, and humans do things together, such as going to church or to the County Fair. White obviously thinks that communities are a bit quaint (in the case of the humans at least), easy to manipulate, and are pleasant to live in. White is no Kipling, however, in perceiving in such groups a tendency toward vulgar or unprincipled behavior. White sees flocks and herds and towns as amusing; like the change of seasons and the smell of manure, groups of creatures, human or otherwise, are an agreeable part of the furniture. But *Charlotte's Web* is in no sense a story about the necessity or even the desirability of finding and belonging to a community. In 1971 White wrote, in a letter to Gene Dietch, who at the time planned to direct a film version of the story: "I think it would be quite untrue to suggest that barnyard creatures are dependent on each other. The barn is a community of rugged individualists, everybody mildly suspicious of everybody else, including me" (*Letters*, 614). This benign fragmentation of groups in *Charlotte's Web* is neither a curse nor a blessing; it is simply, as White's imagination conceives the matter, the way things are.

The more interesting characters in *Charlotte's Web*—Charlotte, Wilbur, and Templeton—do not belong to communities. (When Fern, in the final chapters of the story, makes friends with Henry Fussy and goes to join the human crowd, she essentially makes herself irrelevant to the primary situation, and she disappears.) They are all loners, uncommunitied individualists who remain so to the end of the story. Charlotte and Templeton are, in some respects, symmetrical opposites to each other; symmetrical, in that their situations are remarkably similar; and opposite, in that their behavior within those situations is so different. On one hand, both Charlotte and Templeton are, on the face of it or in human terms, rather disgusting creatures; Charlotte kills insects and drinks their blood, and Templeton eats garbage. On the other hand, unlike the other animals in the story, they are *free*. Wilbur and the other farm animals live in the barn, pens, and pastures because they have to; they are prisoners. Charlotte and Templeton can come and go as they like; if they remain in the barn, it is because they choose to.

Also important, Charlotte and Templeton have skills and talents that are out of the ordinary. Charlotte is an artist or a craftsman; she makes webs, which, in the mythology of this story, is a marvelous, inimitable skill. Templeton, on his side, has hands and manual dexterity; he can tie a string to a pig's tail, he can fetch bits of language or anything else from the dump, and he can play the angles and make bargains as no other animal can.

Finally, both Charlotte and Templeton are hunters or predators, unlike any of the other animals. Unless a hunter belongs to a species that hunts in packs, like wolves, baboons, and some tribes of humans, the nature of a hunter is inherently disposed to antisociability, for other members of a hunter's own species are potential rivals for prey or plunder. Templeton acts in complete accordance with the principle of selfishness implicit in a predator's situation. In considering any project, he asks only one question: What's in it for me? This remains his viewpoint to the end.

As far as her animal nature and the necessities of her life are concerned, Charlotte should be the same way. Spiders do not live in colonies like ants or bees; each spider must (as Charlotte puts it) live by her own wits. (Charlotte points out that there is a social benefit to her killing flies, which are pests to other creatures; but her motives for killing them are not social.) Spiders do not even have family ties to "socialize" them: their mating is not marriage, and, since spiders die before their offspring hatch, they are never parents in the social sense. In and of itself, the spider could well serve as a natural emblem of the solitary life.

In some respects, Charlotte is a spider, in other respects she is a person, and in other respects it is difficult to categorize her. She is definitely a spider in physical details: she has a spider's body and eight legs; she lives on her own, spins webs, catches and drinks the blood of insects; she lays 514 eggs in an egg sac; she lives about one year and dies. She is a person in the following respects: she speaks English very well (indeed, there does not seem to be any such thing as "speaking Spider" in the story); she can read and write; she is (even pedantically) interested in lexicology; she knows the Latin names for the seven sections of a spider's legs. She contemplates life generally and her own in particular, philosophically, and she recognizes that her predatory ways seem sordid from some viewpoints, "something of a mess, with all this trapping and eating flies" (164), and acknowledges the value of raising her life above the purely material and instinctual. Further, she takes a satirical interest in human beings; she exploits their foolish habit of believing anything they see in print, and she laughs at their misguided attempt to build a web, the Queensborough Bridge, that does not catch anything and only encourages people in their unwise impulse to "keep trotting back and forth . . . thinking there is something better on the other side" (60).

SPIDER, FRIEND, SAVIOR

Charlotte's adoption of Wilbur as her friend could belong to either the human or the arachnid side of her nature. One finds instances in nature where animals of one species befriend or adopt animals of another, although the principle seems unlikely to extend as far as spiders bonding with pigs. On the whole, Charlotte's benevolence toward Wilbur is an ideal more human than otherwise.

White claimed that he intended no moral in his story. Advising Dietch on his film adaptation, he wrote: "I do hope, though, that you are not planning to turn 'Charlotte's Web' into a moral tale. It is not that at all. . . . it is essentially amoral, because animals are essentially amoral, and I respect them, and I think this respect is implicit in the tale" (*Letters*, 613). But if Charlotte is not acting on a moral impulse in befriending and saving Wilbur, it is difficult to say what sort of impulse she is acting on. White claimed that he had seen animals of different species form attachments with one another. "Friendships sometimes develop, as between a goat and a horse, but there is no sense of true community or cooperation" (*Letters*, 614). But what Charlotte gives Wilbur is clearly more than this, more than just companionship. A perfectly self-reliant and independent creature herself, she nevertheless sympathizes with a helpless and pathetic pig. A natural killer, she can nevertheless understand killing from the victim's point of view and devote herself to saving a life. Whatever one chooses to call the impulse that motivates her—moral or sentimental or spiritual—Charlotte has plainly risen above her "natural" situation as a spider. She is not so much a friend as she is a savior.

Wilbur, for his part, is pure victim or vulnerable innocent. He is alone not because pigs are loners by nature, but because Homer L. Zuckerman wants to raise just one pig. He has none of the independence or resources of Charlotte and Templeton. He cannot handle freedom (his "escape" in chapter 3 is a fiasco); he cannot cope with captivity by himself. In crises, he becomes hysterical or he faints. When, with Templeton's help, he brings Charlotte's egg sac back from the fair to the barn, he seems to believe he is doing Charlotte or her children a service; but that supposition is punctured when the baby spiders hatch, already perfectly capable of taking care of themselves.

To the friendship with Charlotte, Wilbur brings nothing but need. White hints that there is some kind of reciprocity in Charlotte's and Wilbur's deciding to be friends, as if Wilbur had any real choice in the matter. White flirts with the idea that because of Charlotte's description of her shocking blood-drinking habit, Wilbur might decline her offer of friendship, or that he is taking some sort of "gamble" to accept it. But this is not true. In order to gamble, one must have something to lose, and Wilbur does not. He is despondent with boredom and loneliness, and (we are about to learn) he is to be butchered. Without Charlotte, he has no hope. To accept her help is no gamble.

DEATH TAKES A HOLIDAY

The prospect of death figures significantly in *Charlotte's Web*, not, ultimately, as an eventuality that must be faced, an existential reality, but rather as an unpleasantness to be averted or avoided. White never has to answer St. Paul's rhetorical questions "O death, where is thy sting? O grave, where is thy victory?" because, in this book, "a pig shall be saved."

Charlotte, of course, dies. In a way, the understated account of her passing is the emotional climax of the story, because it is the one place where White treats a serious subject with little lyricism and no humor. The paragraph at the end of chapter 21 where he tells of

Charlotte, the real hero of Wilbur's story, dying alone in a deserted fairgrounds is uniquely sober in this otherwise cheerful story.

Yet it is clear that in some larger perspective, Charlotte's death does not matter. In *Charlotte's Web*, there is only one essential operative question about death: Are you afraid to die? If, as in Charlotte's case, the answer is no, then death is sad, but acceptable. If, on the other hand, as in Wilbur's case, the answer is yes, then death is terrible, unthinkable, unacceptable. Basically, White's storytelling distills the matter of dying down to that one issue—the feelings of the creature who faces it. Other potential questions just do not arise: What implications does the inevitability of death have for the meaning of life? Is there justice or sanctity in death, or is it just a dirty trick that existence plays on us? Is death the extinction of the self, or is it something better? Philosophical questions like these have no place in White's story. Death is either a painless natural phenomenon, as it is for Charlotte, or it is a horrifying atrocity, as it would be for Wilbur.

As the former, there is no need to dread it; as the latter, there is no need to face it.

The story begins with death in the offing: Mr. Arable heads for the hoghouse, ready to dispatch the runt of a too-large litter of pigs. The feelings of the intended victim are not relevant here, because the pig has not become Wilbur yet, presumably has no knowledge of the danger he is in, and so has no reportable reaction. It is Fern who feels threatened and fights back. It is not that she feels sorry for some known, specific creature (she has not even seen the piglets yet); she simply abhors the thought of an innocent little pig being axed to death. She calls the idea "unfair," the "most terrible case of injustice I ever heard of" (3), as if rewards and punishments were somehow at issue here. A more psychologically plausible reason, though, quickly emerges: White suggests that Fern identifies with the victim and on some level imagines the threat as a threat to herself. "If *I* had been very small at birth, would you have killed *me*?" (3). Her father relents—not, one supposes, because he is convinced by Fern's logic that killing little pigs is unjust, but because he sees how terrible a thing it is in her eyes, and he chooses to spare her the pain. (Presumably the next time he has to kill some livestock, he will arrange for Fern to be elsewhere; but he will continue killing.) And so for the first time the pig is saved.

The next death threat to this same pig is much more serious and important to the plot of the story. By this time the pig is Wilbur, a creature with language and personality and a consciousness like the reader's. An old sheep quietly informs him that he is to be butchered at Christmastime.

This information upsets Wilbur extremely, and it is not easy to know the old sheep's motives for telling him. Could she think she is warning Wilbur, so that perchance he might do something to avoid being killed? There is no sign of that; the sheep calls her news "bad," but also describes it as business as usual, "the same thing, same old business, year after year" (49). Does she have some sheeplike inability to imagine how the knowledge of his own imminent death will affect Wilbur? This could be, although she knows enough of its effect to begin by saying she doesn't like to spread bad news and then describes the butchery as a plot and a conspiracy to commit murder—so she clearly understands at least some of the horror of it. To a degree, at least, it appears she tells Wilbur just to be mean, just to torment him. At best, the old sheep is conspicuously callous and indifferent to Wilbur's feelings and, in effect, echoes the lamb's comment from three chapters earlier in the book, that "pigs mean less than nothing to me." The sheep's announcement of the bad news introduces the crucial problem in this story of a pig to be saved; it also helps to establish the fact that although Wilbur may think of himself as having "friends" around the barnyard, Charlotte is the only one who fully sympathizes with him. The others are more like the old sheep: mildly interested, but not deeply concerned.

Wilbur's reaction is natural, spontaneous, and unphilosophical: he screams that he doesn't want to be killed and pleads for somebody to save him (to which the old sheep irritably snaps, "You are certainly making a beautiful noise," as if Wilbur's terror were only an unmannerly breach of the peace of the barnyard). Wilbur says the "reason" he does not want to die is that it would mean taking him away from his comfortable manure pile and the beautiful sun and air and "all my friends"; but the essence of his reaction is instinctive, not rational: he is terrified at the idea of his own extinction.

And this, of course, is what the whole plot of *Charlotte's Web* is designed to excuse him from: "a pig shall be saved." "You shall not die," Charlotte announces firmly (51). Flagrant as this may be as a denial of mortality, in this story it is true. Because of Charlotte's ingenious hoax on the humans, Wilbur never has to die. The end of the story leaves him still alive, still protected, in a kind of permanent state of safety from dying.

The idea that Wilbur is granted a sort of immortality, or rather an immunity to the cycles of birth, maturation, and death that prevail elsewhere or for others, is actually quite fundamental to the imaginative condition of *Charlotte's Web*. White's barnyard here is not A. A. Milne's Hundred-Acre Wood, where no one ever grows old or dies; and neither is it the world of *Little Women* or *The Jungle Books*, where change and death are occurrences that are not only poignant but are also normal as well. The wheel of mortality turns in White's fictional world, but Wilbur is a peculiarly blessed creature, and it does not touch him. Wilbur is young and naive, in need of care when he first emerges as a character; he is young and naive and in need of care as the story ends. He has never had to grow up, to learn or to change, to deal with the world, to work or to sacrifice, or to take responsibility (even for himself). He has only had to accept the generous love of spiders, and his life has been an idyll.

Charlotte, of course, has died; and White asserts that, though her daughters and granddaughters came steadily along to be Wilbur's companions in her place, they never took her place in his heart and he never forgot her. *Remembering* is ineffably important to White. But the blunt fact of the matter is that Charlotte has served her purpose, or carried out her mission, before she dies; she accepts her death uncomplainingly and even with a little expression of relief; and her life and death blend easily with the round of changing seasons to which White frequently refers as the most beautiful of all.

A message of *Charlotte's Web* to its young readers is that they need not worry about dying; that for them to die would be an unnatural horror, which good guardians like Charlotte can prevent; that death is not for the young (like themselves and Wilbur), but for the old, who (like Charlotte) will very likely welcome it when it comes. There is no reason to suppose that White offers these assurances as guarantees or sober realistic appraisals of death in the real world; but they are dependable and plausible enough to provide foundations for his consoling fantasy.

WHY A PIG SHOULD BE SAVED; AND HOW

White's project, recall, was to write a story in which "a pig shall be saved." The conventions of the talking-animal story covered both his essential storytelling problems. They answered two basic questions: Why (in light of the fact that butchery and pork eating are common facts of life) should he be saved? And how is the rescue to be accomplished?

As to why a pig should be saved—*this* pig, Wilbur—the answer is obvious: Wilbur is a person, and a sympathetic person at that. When an animal speaks, in a very fundamental way he *is* a person. The chasm between animal and human, in some sense, disappears. With the power of speech go, implicitly, related faculties: humanlike emotions, a human-style personality, an awareness of the past and the future, and an awareness of oneself as a self, so that the prospect of death—the extinction of that self—is terrifying. In a story like *Charlotte's Web*, creatures who speak the same language as the author and his readers have souls; that is to say, their deaths are just as significant as the death of a human being. (The flies that Charlotte kills do not speak. The whole moral and emotional coherence of *Charlotte's Web* would be lost if White had incidentally shown Charlotte's victims chatting back and forth.)

So White projects a world of animals where death is just as serious as death is in the human world, because animals speak as people do: not in some grunts-and-whistles equivalent to human speech, but exactly as people do.

The "rules" for talking-animal stories vary somewhat from author to author and from story to story. In *The Wind in the Willows* (a story mostly in the "people with animal heads" category), Toad can talk to the human gaoler's daughter and the washerwoman just as well as he can talk to Mole and Rat. In *The Jungle Books* and the Dr. Dolittle series, on the other hand, it takes a special person to translate between humans and animals; left to themselves, humans and animals cannot understand each other at all. The rabbits of *Watership Down* can talk only to rabbits.

The "rule" in *Charlotte's Web* is that animals speak charming English to each other on their side of the fence, and humans converse on their side. The animals understand what people say, and all Fern must do in order to understand the animals is to listen to them. The words that appear in Charlotte's web are in English. So it would seem that animals and humans could talk to each other in this story, as they do in *The Wind in the Willows*.

But they do not. There is apparently a secondary "rule" in *Charlotte's Web*, that animals and humans are not to communicate with each other directly; they are not to speak *to* each other. This turns out to be a crucial rule, insofar as White's idea of *how* a pig shall be saved is concerned. For an animal to direct words toward human beings in this story has to be a kind of miracle, in order for Charlotte's hoax to work. For Fern and for the reader, who know that the animals speak English, the words Charlotte spins in her web are clever and the product of hard work, but they are not miraculous. To all the other humans in the story, they are a miracle, in that they violate some very basic rule or norm of experience.

Recognizing the force of this rule and what a dramatically unusual thing it is for anyone to break it helps to explain what otherwise is a distinct oddity in Charlotte's verbal powers. As a general thing, Charlotte is perfectly articulate, even showily so; she is a fount of impressive language and a smooth and tactful rhetorician. But when it comes to thinking of words to weave into her web in describing Wilbur, she has trouble. Of the four slogans, she produces the first herself: "Some Pig," the least bold and stylish of the series. After that, she seems to suffer writer's block and seeks help from the other animals. It is the goose that proposes "Terrific," and the old sheep has the idea to cajole Templeton into finding words on labels and in newspapers from the dump.

CHARLOTTE'S WRITER'S BLOCK

Why can't Charlotte make up all the slogans herself? My candid guess is that White had at least two practical reasons for creating Charlotte's difficulty. (1) He wanted another scene of interaction between her and the barnyard animals, and this gave him one. White's barnyard is in danger of seeming a socially cold place at times. The more the animals say to each other—and, really, they do not have much to talk about—the more the social atmosphere warms up. (2) The animals' discussion of words for the web makes explicit that they are the language of advertisement and thus underlines White's genial satire. White could have gotten in that point in other ways—by directly telling Charlotte's thoughts, for instance. But he never does that. He frequently reports Wilbur's thoughts and feelings, and sometimes Fern's, and occasionally even Mrs. Arable's and the goose's; but he never explicitly describes what goes on in Charlotte's mind. It is important to understand Charlotte entirely from what she says and does and how other characters react to her. So if the slogans for her web are to be drawn intentionally from advertisements, it is best if someone points it out, as the sheep does in the meeting of the animals.

But those are behind-the-scenes explanations for why Charlotte needs help, comments about what might have gone on in White's mind rather than what happens in the story. Within the story itself, what might explain Charlotte's call for help?

One might argue that she really could think of words for herself, and that she only pretends to be baffled, perhaps as a way of encouraging a helpful and cooperative spirit among the barnyard animals. By acting as if she needs help, one might say, she teaches the animals a little lesson in helpfulness. But this does not seem to be White's conception. Charlotte shows no other sign of wishing to teach the barnyard "community" anything. Her sole interest is in Wilbur, and she interacts with the other animals only insofar as Wilbur's well-being is concerned. Any lesson of mutual help and dependence that she may teach has no discernible effect beyond the present instance; the barnyard is no more and no less communal at the end of the story than it was at the beginning. It remains "the community of rugged individualists, everybody mildly suspicious of everybody else" that White posited at the start. Charlotte's expressed interest has been exclusively in saving Wilbur's life, and in ennobling herself a little by doing it. It makes no compelling sense to suppose that she would pretend to need help doing it, if she did not.

The fact of the matter is that, although White does not explicitly say so, Charlotte will break a basic rule (whether a rule of decorum or a rule of natural possibility is hard to say) in producing words aimed at a human audience. This seems to put some special kind of pressure on her. On all those occasions when Charlotte uses language with such facility, she talks only to animals. Writing to humans, or for them, is a radical step for Charlotte to take. It is something that neither she nor any other animal does, or seems able to do, at any other time in the story.

Actually, Charlotte's project breaks another basic rule: she proposes not to converse with humans, but to deceive them. If her decision were to reveal to the humans that Wilbur is a person (which would presumably lead to the greater revelation that all the animals are people), and therefore that to kill him would be murder, presumably her web-words would be very different: something like "Wilbur has a soul!" or "Meat is murder!" But she proposes to leave people in their misconception that animals are mere things, and to save Wilbur by convincing them that he is a wonderful thing, a thing worth saving. Again, this is an event unique in the story. Nobody, not even Templeton, lies to, misleads, or tricks anybody in *Charlotte's Web*—except Charlotte.

It is perhaps understandable, then, that she is unusually nervous about her choice of words on this occasion. She is doing something that is doubly unfamiliar to her: she is forming words for a human audience, and she is using language to foster a deception. It is appropriate that she might want some support in this extraordinarily bold and possibly hazardous enterprise. (Would something terrible happen if humans had to face the fact that animals could talk?) For once she calls on the other animals to rally around and help her. Even for so confident and competent a creature as Charlotte, this "unnatural" stroke of wordplay is too portentous to undertake entirely alone. She wants to share the responsibility with others. (I think it is unlikely that White consciously thought of it this way; but it does fit the "facts" of the story.)

A Good Writer

The passage most often quoted from *Charlotte's Web* is its last two sentences: "It is not often that someone comes along who is a true friend and a good writer. Charlotte was both." These words are among the most famous in all of children's literature.

In his study of the versions and revisions that White went through in writing *Charlotte's Web*, Peter Neumeyer notes that these soon-to-be-famous words were not an inspired afterthought but were already present in White's first full draft of the story. Well before he knew how he was going to begin the tale, White knew he was going to end it with those sentences.

The sentences are an odd twist. That Charlotte has been a true friend to Wilbur, and that this is a fact crucial in the story, is unmistakable; it is a touching note on which to end the narrative. But in declaring Charlotte a "good writer," White does something odd, and he provides a playful, ironic, *New Yorker*–ish touch that has the effect, and presumably the purpose, of deflating, just a little, the sentimental mood in which the story ends.

Some of the same effect could have been achieved with closing words on Charlotte, other than that she was a good writer. "It is not often that a pig is blessed with a true friend who has twice as many legs as he has. But Wilbur was blessed." Or "some people think that neither a pig nor a spider is worthy of love. But that is because they never knew Wilbur and Charlotte." But with his last rhetorical flour-

ish, White turns away from Charlotte's spiderhood and eulogizes her
as a writer.

She really has not been much of a writer, of course. Her entire
literary canon consists of the five famous words in her web: "Some
Pig," "Terrific," "Radiant," and "Humble." She needed help in choos-
ing three of those five. And of White's two cardinal points of stylistic
excellence—brevity and clarity—Charlotte scores well only for brevity. Clarity has never been her objective; as would a canny advertising
copywriter, she has wanted suggestiveness, connotation, and overtone,
with a nice hazy place at the center. Is Wilbur really "some pig," "radiant," and "terrific"? The story establishes that if you think he is, he
is—but probably not otherwise.

It is not so much the content of what Charlotte writes that saves
Wilbur, as that she writes at all. Once the device has been established
of promoting Wilbur's value, or hyping him, with words in the web,
any number of terms and slogans would do equally well. White's draft
notes show that he toyed with several himself: "pig of distinction,"
"prepotent," "worth more," and so forth. "Fine pig," "wonderful,"
"unique," "noble," "vital," "classy"—potentially, Charlotte's options
are limitless. It does not matter very much what she writes, as long as
she writes—and convinces people that her words apply to Wilbur.

Basically it is in the nature of an inside joke that White calls
Charlotte a good writer: a smiling acknowledgment that White himself
was a writer and that some of his friends were writers. Joseph Epstein
proposes that White was thinking of his wife Katharine when he wrote
the words.[4] But White had a gallery of author-friends who might also
see themselves reflected in the comment.

For those who are aware of White's career beyond children's literature—the concluding sentences serve gently to break the pretense
that White is passionately concerned with this pig and this spider, and
to remind them that he is an urbane and successful literary wit, well
connected in the world of writers.

For people who do not know anything about White except that
he wrote *Charlotte's Web* and maybe *Stuart Little*, but who do think
about what words say—that final claim that Charlotte was a good
writer is probably laughed off as White's good-natured insertion of a

tribute to good writers where one does not logically belong. Or it could prompt one to consider whether Charlotte *is* in some less-than-obvious sense a good writer, even though she hardly ever writes.

What Charlotte has been, more than a good writer, is a good talker. All of her dealings with Wilbur have been entirely through spoken words; there is absolutely no physical contact between them. She has entertained him, educated him, directed him, soothed him, teased him, scolded him, and advised him—all with her words. If "good writer" can be taken as a near-synonym for "skilled user of language" or "wordsmith," then probably Charlotte has earned her epithet.

It may be significant, though, that Charlotte really is not a good storyteller. Just as deception seemed to be difficult for her, so does fiction. In chapter 13 Wilbur begs for a bedtime story. Charlotte does not want to tell one, but she yields to Wilbur's request. She knows enough about stories to begin "Once upon a time"; but what she actually provides are a couple of odd facts about her cousin who once caught a fish in her web and who was a balloonist. Her account of the battle with the fish contains a little action-description parodying a prize-fight announcer—"Then a left to the tail and a right to the midsection" (103)—but ends very flatly. Wilbur asks what finally happened. "Nothing," says Charlotte, dispassionately informing him that her cousin subdued the fish and eventually ate it. The "story" of the cousin's balloon travels is two sentences long. Clearly, Charlotte is not nearly so good or enthusiastic a storyteller as White was. It may be part of White's conception of Charlotte's animal nature (the same trait in her that made it hard for her to work up a deception on the humans—not moral scruples, but a lack of natural inclination or talent) that she is not good at fabricating pseudotruth, a story.

Sometimes when readers asked White about his depiction of barnyard life in *Charlotte's Web,* or of the behavior of swans in *The Trumpet of the Swan,* he had an odd way of claiming it was all very true to life, very realistic. "I discovered that there was no need to tamper in any way with the habits and characteristics of spiders, pigs, geese, and rats" (*Letters,* 613). Obviously, this is not the whole truth about a story where spiders, pigs, geese, and rats chat about life and death, confer over what words should be woven into a web, and so on.

But it probably says something about what White saw or meant in the basic rule that humans and animals do not normally exchange words with each other. That the words (and personalities) of animals almost never crack through into the awareness of human beings in his story is probably a literary correlative for the real-life difference between humans and animals. That such a breakthrough occurs once, on Homer L. Zuckerman's farm, to persuade him not to butcher a pig named Wilbur—that is the privilege of fantasy that White obviously claimed for himself.

A pig shall be saved, decided White, because (in *Charlotte's Web*) a pig is a person, and because another not-human person, a spider, bends the rules, risks exposing her personhood to the human world by using words for them to see, and plays a trick that works.

6

On Nature

WRITING ABOUT ANIMALS

White approached the writing of children's stories as a confessed amateur, a man who had earned his spurs as an essayist and writer of light verse and humor pieces but who was relatively ignorant of the conventions of juvenile literature. White had had literary interests since childhood, to be sure. He knew that he might want to be a writer as early as the age of nine, when he determined to keep a journal and write something in it every day; he won a prize from *Woman's Home Companion* for a poem about a mouse that he wrote when he was 10; he won a literary prize from *St. Nicholas Magazine* when he was 11 and another when he was 14. Still, reading children's literature does not seem to have been particularly important for White when he was a child.

At any rate, when he turned to writing children's stories as a man, he presented himself as a rank outsider. Shortly after submitting the manuscript of *Charlotte's Web* to Ursula Nordstrom, editor of children's books at Harper's, he asked her if she "had ever encountered any story plot like 'Charlotte's Web'—that is, any case in fiction of a spider writing words in its web. I'm not well read in juvenile literature, or any other kind, and am always fearful that I have unwittingly created something that has already been done by somebody else" (*Letters*, 353). Nordstrom responded—facetiously, one assumes—with the legend of Robert the Bruce, who was inspired to rise and fight again by the sight of a spider diligently spinning its web.

Obviously White was aware that children's fiction permitted a latitude of fantasy not usually claimed by writers for adults; he knew that it is a good idea to include a child as a protagonist as well. Beyond that, he does not seem to have had any particular theory about what a children's story should be. Casually looking over the huge crop of new children's books that his wife was reviewing for the *New Yorker* in 1938, White had the tone and attitude of a stranger in the land of juvenile literature. "I have naturally come to know something about children's books from living so close to them and gazing hatefully at their jackets," he wrote (*OMM*, 28). Still, he decided, "it must be a lot of fun to write for children—reasonably easy work, perhaps even important work." Rather than setting out to emulate any particular children's author, or to write a story in a certain genre, White seems to have felt his way, intuitively, toward the conventions that suited him in *Charlotte's Web*. With his first children's story, *Stuart Little*, published seven years earlier, he had (according to his own account) "followed my instincts," which "seemed to be the way a writer should operate."[1] With *Charlotte's Web*, he followed them again.

White's love of animals was unmistakably an important source of inspiration for *Charlotte's Web*. By his own report, White had an intense affinity for animals from his childhood on. In an autobiographical article called "A Boy I Knew," White wrote of himself (in the third person): "This boy felt for animals a kinship he never felt for people. Against considerable opposition and with woefully inadequate equipment, he managed to provide himself with animals, so that he would never be without something to tend." He remembered keeping "pigeons, dogs, snakes, polliwogs, turtles, rabbits, lizards, singing birds, chameleons, caterpillars and mice." He spent uncounted hours "just standing watching animals, or refilling their water pans . . . ; and it would be hard to say what he got out of it."[2]

His delight in having a menagerie to tend seems never to have abated. He owned a number of dogs and other pets over the course of his life; and when, in 1938, he moved to a small salt-water farm in Maine, he stocked it with sheep, cattle, chickens, pigs, and geese. He also took pleasure in observing the behavior of wild creatures on his farm—raccoons, skunks, foxes, birds, and so forth. He said the farm was more of a zoo than a farm.

WHICH KIND OF STORY IS *CHARLOTTE'S WEB*?

White's feeling about animals seems to have been an unusual mixture of the naturalist's love of pure observation, the farmer's businesslike concern for care, feeding, and harvesting, and the pet-lover's pleasure in animals' companionship, enriched by a certain imaginative projection onto them of human personalities. *Charlotte's Web* contains signs of all these attitudes, and (perhaps as a result) it falls somewhere in between the major categories of animal stories. White did considerable reading about the lives of spiders in preparing to write his book, in order to make his depiction of Charlotte broadly accurate from an arachnological point of view. But obviously *Charlotte's Web* does not belong with nature-study stories like Felix Salten's *Bambi* (1929) or Walt Morey's *Gentle Ben* (1965). Though Charlotte's spider background may be good natural history, what makes her story worth telling is her most "unnatural" feat of spinning words in her web.

Neither, obviously, does *Charlotte's Web* belong with pet stories like Sheila Burnford's *An Incredible Journey* (1961) or Will James's *Smoky, the Cow Horse* (1926)—stories in which love between people and animals is always central. Although Wilbur starts out as Fern's pet in this conventional sense, White's story quickly moves to a different focus entirely, and it becomes in the end what might be called an antipet story, in that it lovingly posits a set of animal relationships from which human beings are entirely absent.

ANIMALS IN WONDERLANDS

Because the primary characters in *Charlotte's Web* are animals that talk, White's story is usually categorized as fantasy of the talking-animal variety—and rightly so. But it should be noted what limited use White makes of his license for the fantastic. When one compares *Charlotte's Web* with other classics of the talking-animal kind, such as *The Wind in the Willows*, the *Just-So Stories*, and the Beatrix Potter books, one realizes how modestly White has humanized his animal characters, and how soberly he has kept his eye on real-life barnyards in creating his fictional world. Despite the prominence of talking animals in it, *Charlotte's Web* in some respects has as much kinship with realistic stories like *The Adventures of Tom Sawyer*, *Little House on the Prairie*, and *The Moffats* as with most other talking-animal fantasies.

Often, talking animals belong to fictional worlds that are quite fanciful—whole projected realms or alternative planes of existence in which the speech of animals is only one of many improvements on reality. Animals talk in L. Frank Baum's land of Oz, in C. S. Lewis's Narnia, in Lewis Carroll's Wonderland—and a great many other wonders happen in those places as well. Baum, Lewis, and Carroll, more than just telling stories, created fantasy worlds. Having read these authors at length, one remembers not so much specific things that happen in their books, but rather the "magic" in the land itself, the ways in which life there goes on differently. With such worlds, authors can write sequels; the worlds themselves have possibilities that can be developed and explored in additional episodes. A primary pleasure in reading such fiction is the pleasure of entering their worlds—and reentering them, as often as the author is willing to grant admission.

Likewise, Rudyard Kipling created a sort of wonderland in his *Just-So Stories*—only he called it a wonder *time*, "the High and Far-Off Times" in "the beginning of years, when the world was so new and all"[3]—a time when comically mythic things happened, producing camels' humps, elephants' trunks, and rhinoceroses' wrinkly skins, which can still be seen at the zoo. And Kipling created another wonderland in the jungle of the Seeonee Hills in India, where Mowgli comes to live with a wolf-family and Bagheera the panther and Baloo the bear. For both of these milieux, wonders peculiar to them go on and on, limited apparently only by Kipling's having the time and inclination to tell them. Theoretically there is no end to the oddities of animal and human existence that Kipling could explain in his witty, poetic, visionary *Just-So* manner. And the unique mixture of chivalric heroism and animal ways that Kipling contrived for the *Jungle Books* is likewise extensible, as Edgar Rice Burroughs demonstrated when he took over many of them for his *Tarzan* series.

Kenneth Grahame never wrote a sequel to *The Wind in the Willows*, but he surely could have, without doing violence to the original. (Dixon Scott has in fact done it, in *A Fresh Wind in the Willows*, 1983.) Life goes on, on Grahame's riverbank, in Toad Hall, and in the Wild Woods, in ways that could be extended and developed appropriately. More outings, more boat trips, more chummy conversations, more shenanigans from Toad (who patently has not really reformed at the end of the story, not in his heart), more encounters with weasels, stoats, foxes, or other as-yet-undiscovered Wild Wooders, are all imaginable. Grahame's fantasy world has room to walk around in.

BARNYARD OF LIMITED WONDERS

But the world of *Charlotte's Web* does not have room to walk around in. It is true that White seems to have thought of his story as being about "a world." He liked to call it "a report from the barn cellar, which I love dearly" (*Letters*, 614). And many of White's readers have praised the story for its rich and vivid evocation of the farm as an Edenic setting. But White's barnyard is clearly not a world of its own in the same way that those other story-places are. Zuckerman's barn is not a place where endless stories happen; it is (by definition) an ordinary, mundane place where *one* story happens: writing appears in a spider's web. To try to exploit White's barnyard for further wonders would collapse the balance of fantasy and realism that he has engineered. What more could happen that would be both dramatic and in the spirit of what is already in *Charlotte's Web*? A goose could become a concert singer? (White attempted something of that sort in *The Trumpet of the Swan*, with results unworthy of *Charlotte's Web*.) Templeton the rat could go hunting for treasure or become a spy for the CIA? One returns to Zuckerman's barn not for adventures but for peace. The place is not even apparently magic without Charlotte, and Charlotte has fulfilled her one mission in life and died, as she had to do.

In a sense, White creates a world (or, as he would probably prefer to say, records or reports one that he has found in the barn) in much the same way that Mark Twain created (or recorded or reported) a world in *Tom Sawyer* or Louisa May Alcott created one in *Little Women*: a world of details about life fondly recalled and selected. Twain and Alcott, having established their respective ambiences of playful and sober possibilities and the natures of their characters, can simply show those natures in action, and some of those possibilities achieved, confident that life within the norms of their fiction is compelling and significant. White, on the other hand, uses up the world he has made, by employing it as the setting for a miracle that, for obvious reasons, cannot be repeated without destroying the central dramatic effect. For White, farm life is interesting and lovable, but rises to the level of story-material only as the backdrop for Charlotte's master stroke of breaking through the norms.

THE MOMENT THE ANIMALS SPOKE

Amid the various kinds of talking-animal stories that abound in children's literature, *Charlotte's Web* belongs to a special subcategory: the tradition of stories about the dramatic moment when animals, who have been conversing among themselves all along, cross over a line and make contact with humans. The Mowgli stories in the *Jungle Books* belong to this tradition; they project a world in which humans converse with each other, and animals converse with each other, but only when Mowgli comes along and happens to fall in with the animals at a very early age does any human being learn the animals' language. Selma Lagerlöf's *The Wonderful Adventures of Nils* (1907) tells of a Swedish boy who, when he is magically reduced to the size of an elf, begins to understand the language of geese, cats, and other animals. *The Story of Dr. Dolittle* (1920), about a doctor who studies and learns the language of animals by a special devotion to the task, is one of the most famous works in this tradition. George Selden's *The Cricket in Times Square* (1960) develops a variation of the basic situation when a cricket named Chester becomes famous among humans because he can chirp classical music, and again in *Tucker's Countryside* (1969), where Tucker the mouse dupes some humans by gnawing letters in a signboard. Nathaniel Benchley's *Kilroy and the Gull* (1977) is about a killer whale who, with great effort, finally succeeds in communicating with humans. One could add other examples, though the list would never be very long.

ANIMALS, PEOPLE, AND NATURE

The story that focuses on the special time when animals speak to people, or on the moment when a person first understands animal speech, places its author within a certain range of attitudes toward nature and people's place in it. Tellers of stories about animals that talk only to each other and operate in a world exclusively or primarily animal (e.g., *Bambi*, *Watership Down*, *Mrs. Frisby and the Rats of NIMH*) can show great and knowing interest in natural animal life, and they may incidentally locate their animals' experiences in some relation to humanity (as when Hazel's band encounters the man-tended rabbit warren in *Watership Down*, with its morbid dependence on humans who exact rabbit-lives in exchange for their "protection"); but the general effect of such stories is to suggest, by a variety of imaginative means, that nonhuman lives are interesting and important in themselves, and that humanity is a dispensable subject.

At another extreme are the talking-animal stories in which some or all of the characters are what Margaret Blount calls "people with animal heads"—creatures whose animal qualities are limited to a few features of size and appearance: the White Rabbit, the March Hare, and the Caterpillar in *Alice in Wonderland*, for instance; or the Fox, the Cat, and the Talking Cricket in *The Adventures of Pinocchio*; or, for that matter, the frog in "The Frog Prince" or Beast in "Beauty and the Beast." Such stories may, in some faint or roundabout way, express attitudes toward animal life; but it is by no means certain or obvious that they do. The animals are animals in such stories not because the teller has something primary to say about rabbits, crickets, or frogs, but because of other symbolic and stylistic considerations.

In stories about the time when animals speak to humans, however, it is important that, to some extent or in some basic ways, the animals truly are animals; otherwise the fact that they manage to speak to people, or that people manage to understand them, is of no importance. And since the animals in such stories "really are animals," their authors inevitably project some idea, or some intuition, or some feeling, about the relation between the planes of animal and human life; between "animal instinct" and "human reason"; between the primal and the artificial; between nature and civilization. The very notion that there is something dramatically interesting about verbal communication across a gap that, in ordinary life, is seldom or never bridged implies that the author finds something significant in the problematic relation between humanity and nature.

WHITE AND NATURE

If you had asked White how he felt about nature, there is little doubt that he would have said he loved and respected it. In some moods, he would say he worshiped it. Referring to himself in the third person, he once wrote: "He was saddled with an unusual number of worries, it seems to me, but faith underlay them—a faith nourished by the natural world rather than by the supernatural or spiritual" ("A Boy," 34). He could think of the observation of nature as a kind of religious ceremony. "There was a lake, and at the water's edge a granite rock upholstered with lichen. This was his pew, and the sermon went on forever." In such moods, White's thoughts could become uncharacter-istically metaphysical, expressing "the haunting intimation (which I presume every child receives) of his mystical inner life; of God in man; of nature publishing herself through the 'I'" (*OMM*, 208). It is uncer-tain how constant was his "sense of identification with the natural company of insects and grass and night," and how often he could hear "a faint answering cry to the universal perplexing question: `What is `I'?" (*OMM*, 208). But he testifies to some familiarity with those feel-ings in his writing.

White would also say that fear was an element in his feeling toward nature. This was perhaps most true of his feeling for the sea. As a youth, he hated and feared the sea, he wrote, but felt compelled to swim and sail in it anyway; later "I found that what I had feared and hated, I now feared and loved."[4] As a boy, he said he fearfully but will-ingly went out in "squalls and thunderstorms, rain and darkness, alone in rented canoes." He "swam from the rocks of Hunter's Island, often at night, making his way there alone and afraid . . ." ("A Boy," 35). If in his mystical mood he had a sense of uplifting identification with nature and "a faith nourished by the natural world," in this other mood, in fearful confrontation with storm and night and the sea, he seems also to have had a real and perhaps primal sense of nature as Other, a vital force or presence different from humanity and potential-ly inimical to it.

White's literary hero Thoreau used to praise wildness. "Give me wildness whose glance no civilization can endure," he wrote in the essay "Walking"—"as if we lived on the marrow of koodoos devoured raw."[5] Kenneth Grahame may have had something comparable in mind when he told of "the Terror of the Wild Wood" that falls on Mole when he brashly enters a wilderness "that lay before him low and threatening, like a black reef in some still southern sea."[6] White himself once wrote an essay that brought him close to the subject of a threatening or unendurable wildness—a piece called "Coon Hunt," for his "One Man's Meat" department in *Harper's*. In the essay, White tells of his going out, for the first time in his life, to hunt coon at night with some of his Maine neighbors. The hunters bring along an experi-enced coon-hunting dog, and also a puppy that has never hunted before. White describes the puppy's nervous excitement throughout the expedition—"he was trembling in every muscle, and was all eyes and ears and nose—like a child being allowed to see something meant only for grownups. (I felt a little that way myself.)" (*OMM*, 333). Late in the hunt, the young dog goes temporarily insane, maddened (White surmises) by "the deep dark woods, big with imaginary coons and enormous jealous old hounds, alive with the beautiful smells of the wild. His evening had been too much for him; for the time being he was as crazy as a loon" (*OMM*, 335).

A Kipling, a Stevenson, or a Jack London might have found in the image of a young dog gone mad at his first encounter with the wilderness the sounding of some moral, spiritual, or instinctual depth unavailable to civilization, perhaps subversive to it. White's approach is to defuse the experience by gently humanizing it. He compares the puppy to a child who has been allowed to stay up too late and gotten overtired and overexcited. He ends his essay by assuring the reader that the puppy was all right. "All he needed was to be held in somebody's arms. He was very, very sleepy. He and I were both sleepy. I think we will both remember the first night we ever went coon hunting" (*OMM*, 338).

White, then, knew something of Thoreau's "wildness" and Grahame's "Terror of the Wild Woods," but he was not much given to contemplating them. Far more characteristic of his comments on nature would be, for example, his *New Yorker* paragraph about a sparrow he observed, which found "a small length of blue confetti tied in a bow" and flew around for a time looking "as though he had on an outsize Windsor tie" (*Writings*, 5); or his observation of a raccoon on his Maine farm: "In the tree she seems dainty and charming; the circles under her eyes make her look slightly dissipated and deserving of sympathy. The moment she hits the ground, all this changes; she seems predatory, sinister, and as close to evil as anything in Nature (which contains no evil) can be." He rounds off the passage with a joke: "If I were an Indian, naming animals, I would call the raccoon He Who Has the Perpetual Hangover."[7]

In such evocations of nature, one senses neither terror nor a mystical uplifting faith. Rather, White half-humorously and half-seriously projects human qualities on bits of animal behavior. The confidence and comfort with which he does so implies a sense of kinship between humans and animals that he probably really believes in. The fact that he finds humor or other congenial sentiments in offering his observations implies that he expects his readers to be a little surprised by them, but receptive.

Viewed in this light that reveals quaint resemblances between animal and human life, or a genial correspondence between an observer's mood and the landscape he looks on—nature is a relatively tame and quiet thing, neither terrifying nor rapturously inspirational. Philosophically, White's view seems close to William Cullen Bryant's, in the opening lines of "Thanatopsis"[8]:

> To him who in the love of Nature holds
> Communion with her visible forms, she speaks
> A various language; for his gayer hours
> She has a voice of gladness, and a smile
> And eloquence of beauty, and she glides
> Into his darker musings, with a mild
> And healing sympathy, that steals away
> Their sharpness, ere he is aware.

NATURE IN *CHARLOTTE'S WEB*

Nature in *Charlotte's Web* takes this domesticated form, speaking with "a voice of gladness" for the "gayer hours," and offering "a mild and healing sympathy" for the "darker musings" on death and loneliness. Nature here is Charlotte and the goose laying their eggs, proud and officious as human parents. It is the sun coming up on the farm, the lilacs and apple trees blossoming in early summer, the birds singing "Cheeky, cheeky" and "Oh, Peabody, Peabody, Peabody." At its least friendly, it is the thermometer dropping to ten degrees below zero, so that the animals stay closer to the barn, and Wilbur plows the drifts in his yard, "for the fun of it," and Fern and Avery go sledding.

White's crickets do sing of death. "They sang the song of summer's ending, a sad, monotonous song. 'Summer is over and gone,' they sang. 'Over and gone, over and gone. Summer is dying, dying'"

(113). The song sparrows know that life is lovely but brief, and sing "Sweet, sweet, sweet interlude" (43). But the only death that actually occurs in the story is Charlotte's, a peaceful, unresisted passing. By and large, nature in *Charlotte's Web* is a serene and amiable process, significant primarily for the way it underlines and confirms the pleasantness of the farm and the safety it provides against unnamed sad possibilities that may exist out there somewhere beyond its boundaries.

Norton Kinghorn has found in this an Edenic view of nature; he sees in "the life of the barn, the life of all of nature, of the changing seasons,"[9] an out-and-out Paradise, a state of innocence before the fall. Perhaps he is right; but, if so, this is an Eden peculiarly domesticated as a farm, and shaded with the pensive consciousness of mutability and loss that is foreign to most Edens.

What then does White make of "the moment the animals spoke"? What spaces and connections between animals and humans does his story assume? Actually, in *Charlotte's Web*, the connections are strong and the spaces are small. The difference between animal life and human life here is not nearly so great as in the Mowgli stories or in *The Wonderful Adventures of Nils*. White's animals are pretty nearly human—slightly simplified, slightly purified humans with different eating habits and no clothes. They are domesticated, both literally and figuratively. Even Templeton, the ostensibly antisocial rat, has bought into the system by the end of the story; he takes his meals from Wilbur's trough and grows hugely fat and sedentary.

White's animals easily understand human words and actions; reciprocally, Fern understands the animals. Other humans in the story casually accept the possibility, if not the established fact, that animals talk. "Maybe they do talk," says Fern's father. "I've sometimes wondered" (54). "It is quite possible that an animal has spoken civilly to me and that I didn't catch the remark because I wasn't paying attention," says Dr. Dorian (110). Poor Mrs. Arable with her exaggerated concern over Fern's report of animal conversations seems to be the only person who is bothered by the idea of talking animals. But then she has serious difficulty in accepting the obvious: during her visit to Dr. Dorian, she both complains that animals could not possibly talk the way Fern says they do and puzzles over the words that have been appearing in a spider's web. Somehow she fails to see that Fern's reports and the words in the web confirm one another.

When all is said and done, what most fundamentally distinguishes animal life from human life in *Charlotte's Web* is its regularity, dependability, and serenity. Human life in the story is not especially hectic or hard driven or *un*serene. Charlotte says it is—"With men it's rush, rush, rush, every minute. I'm glad I'm a sedentary spider" (60)—but the behavior of the human characters does not particularly bear her out. Still, animal life is eminent for its tranquility here: "the garrulous geese, the changing seasons . . . the sameness of sheep, the love of spiders, the smell of manure, and the glory of everything" (183).

Charlotte's Web is about "the moment the animals spoke"; and that means it is also about the animals that are always speaking, quietly and patiently and unchangingly. In White's vision, human beings could treat themselves to very soothing interludes if they would just sit down near animals and pay attention—as White himself was accustomed to doing, both as man and boy. He thought of farm life generally as valuable for its calm. "I am always carrying something—a burdensome life, but kind of soothing," he wrote in a letter. "My sheep are soothing, too. They come up out of the pasture at this time of year and stand around in the barn, and that is very soothing to me, to see sheep standing around, waiting" (*Letters*, 201).

Walt Whitman spoke for E. B. White when he said "I think I could turn and live with animals, they / are so placid and self-contain'd, / I stand and look at them long and long" ("Song of Myself").

THOREAU

White's one towering literary hero, the one major author whose life and work he repeatedly praised in print, was Henry David Thoreau. White felt a kinship in spirit with Thoreau, for three reasons: (1) Thoreau loved the woods, the fields, and the out-of-doors; so did White. (2) Thoreau was a humorist who subtly and persistently satirized the vanities of materialism, progressivism, and social conformity; so, in his way, did White. (3) As a writer, Thoreau specialized in the well-crafted witty sentence or small group of sentences rather than the extended argument or developed philosophical system; so did White. White admired, for instance, Thoreauvian sentences like these: "This farmer is endeavoring to solve the problem of a livelihood by a formula more complicated than the problem itself. To get his shoestrings he speculates in herds of cattle" (Quoted in White, *Essays*, 240). In Thoreau, White saw a witty and stylish American writer who praised nature, criticized fads and fashions, wrote saucy aphoristic prose, and claimed to have found the meaning of life in simple, rustic enterprises. In all these respects, White found common ground with Thoreau.

But there were numerous respects in which White was profoundly unlike Thoreau, both as a man and as a writer.

For one thing, as White well knew, in embracing Thoreau's principle of "simplicity," White diluted or otherwise altered it drastically. Thoreau's ideal of the simple life was truly radical; Thoreau was celibate and abstinent, distrustful of material possessions of every kind. White, on the other hand (as Scott Elledge puts it) "was aware, of course, that he could not himself be satisfied by Thoreau's 'existence without material adornment.' He had only to remember his need for Old Town canoes, and Model T Fords, and twenty-foot catboats—to say nothing of his need for a wife and a family and a saltwater farm" (314).

The difference between White's attitude and Thoreau's attitude toward physical, social, and domestic "adornment" is not casual or superficial, but part of a difference in mind-sets that is fundamental. Another way to characterize that basic difference is to point out that Thoreau's tart social and moral criticism appeared primarily in his private journals; in the little magazine the *Dial*, a transcendentalist journal with a circulation of a few hundred; in lectures at the Concord, Massachusetts, Lyceum; in books like *Walden*, which hardly anyone bought during Thoreau's lifetime; and in the *Atlantic Monthly* when it was starting out as an intellectual journal with an abolitionist platform. E. B. White, on the other hand, printed his witty social commentary in the pages of the *New Yorker*, a chic and stylish magazine of arts and entertainment for the urban and the urbane.

One of White's first *New Yorker* pieces, in 1925, was about White's having a glass of buttermilk spilled on his blue suit in Child's

Restaurant on Fifth Avenue, and his Chaplinesque efforts to maintain his dignity through the debacle. This points to another basic contrast between White and Thoreau: Thoreau was a humorist, but he took *himself* with utmost seriousness. Thoreau's satiric humor is directed entirely against that which he found absurd in other people; he is never the butt of his own jokes. White, on the other hand, frequently cultivated the persona of an antihero, a "mousy, faintly worried little man," a "hack writer," a "clown of average ability," as he sometimes called himself.

Thoreau was thoroughly literary. Educated in the old classical tradition at Harvard, he read voraciously in ancient and modern literature; his writing is dense with quotations from and allusions to classical myth, poetry and philosophy, the Bible, the Bhagavad-Gita, Confucius, Shakespeare, Milton, and a range of Renaissance and eighteenth- and nineteenth-century poets and dramatists. Thoreau wrote as if he were already a member of the pantheon of literary and philosophical immortals, speaking their language and addressing their questions. White, on the other hand, almost never used literary, mythic, or historical allusions. Scott Elledge notes that, after Thoreau, White's literary idols were "New York wits" such as Robert Benchley, Dorothy Parker, Franklin P. Adams, Alexander Woollcott, and others of their circle (100).

The worlds of Thoreau's imagination and White's touch only at certain points, and sometimes the juxtaposition is revealing. For instance, in the essay "A Slight Sound at Evening," one of his tributes to Thoreau, White compared *Walden* to "an invitation to life's dance, assuring the troubled recipient that no matter what befalls him in the way of success or failure he will always be welcome at the party—that the music is played for him, too, if he will but listen and move his feet." White proposed that Thoreau's book is "an invitation, unengraved; and it stirs one as a young girl is stirred by her first big party bid" (*Essays*, 234–35). White offers this comparison—*Walden* as an invitation to a debutante's ball—not as a deeply considered "reading" of Thoreau's masterpiece, but as the way *Walden* struck him when he read it as a young man. Nevertheless, one must notice by what an unThoreauvian metaphor White summarizes Thoreau: life is a party and a dance—images loaded with all the connotations of frivolity and empty sociability that Thoreau despised.

One could say that for White the music of life was written in an entirely different key or tonality from what Thoreau heard. Life produced emotional experiences for White that were entirely missing from Thoreau's reports, and vice versa. Consider, for example, this passage from *One Man's Meat*: "A man gets homesick for the loneliness that he has at one time or another experienced in his life and that is part of all life in some degree," wrote White; "sometimes a secluded and half-mournful yet beautiful place will suddenly revive the sensation of pain and melancholy and unfulfillment that are associated with that loneliness, and will make him want to seize and recapture it." He concludes by recalling the importance of wife and family: "I know with me it is a passing want and not to be compared with my taste for domesticity, which is most of the time so strong as to be overpowering" (296). Homesickness, nostalgia, loneliness—and the compensatory craving for domesticity—are all states of mind that Thoreau's writing never evokes, and White's frequently does.

Thoreau's roots were deep in the stern, austere spirituality and moralism of New England Puritanism. Although he was unchurched and could in no sense be called an orthodox Christian, Thoreau's thinking is pervaded by a belief in the ultimacy of spiritual reality and in moral absolutes. This is foreign to E. B. White. What was wrong with society, in Thoreau's view, was that it had lost God. What was wrong with society, for White, was that it tended to make him anxious and depressed. The basic difference between White's moral stance and Thoreau's is exemplified by a piece called "On a Florida Key," which White wrote for "One Man's Meat." White tells of attending a racially segregated movie theater in a small Florida town, and being struck by the irony that an all-white audience applauded the image, on the screen, of an American flag and the words "one nation, indivisible, with liberty and justice for all." White says he "sat there wondering what would happen to me if I were to jump up and say in a loud voice: 'If you folks like liberty and justice so much, why do you keep Negroes from this theater?'" He feels sure "it would have surprised people very much and it is the kind of thing I dream about doing but never do"

(*Essays*, 139). Thoreau would have done it; Thoreau was always doing things like that.

The point is not that Thoreau had the courage of his convictions and White lacked it. The point is that their hearts and minds were really in quite different places. The poet Adrienne Rich once wrote that she thought "without detracting an inch from H. D. T., that it must be a good deal more difficult to be E. B. White in the 20th century than Henry Thoreau in the 19th" (Elledge, 315). White was unmistakably a twentieth-century figure, just as surely as Thoreau was a man of the nineteenth. For White, the philosophic certainties in which Thoreau wholeheartedly believed were not really available, whether or not he had been of the temperament to seek them.

7

The Fable

WHITE'S BASIC FABLE

White wrote three books for children: *Stuart Little* (1945), *Charlotte's Web* (1952), and *The Trumpet of the Swan* (1970). Different as are the details of their plots, all three are, deep down, versions of the same story: the story of an odd little creature, good-hearted and potentially a bit pathetic, born into a world shaped for others who are not like him. Stuart Little is a child who looks exactly like a mouse, born into a family of normal humans. Wilbur is the runt of his litter, narrowly saved from being disposed of as a nuisance and consigned to a life without the society of his own kind in a world controlled by humans. Louis is a trumpeter swan born mute, lacking the voice that is the special mark of his species and ordinarily its only way of communicating.

In broad terms, the problem for Stuart, Wilbur, and Louis is to find or contrive some accommodation to the normal world so that they can live lives with most of the satisfactions of normality. White's basic fable is not that of "The Ugly Duckling," where the oddities of the little hero turn out, in the natural course of events, to be the precursors of his excellence. And neither is it the fable of the old folk fairy tales, where the youngest of a set of brothers or sisters appears at the beginning to lack promise, but in the course of the story demonstrates wit, beauty, or goodness that makes him or her the most valued of the family.

In White's basic fable, the hero does not win the race that the society around him runs. Rather he finds a different race in which he is the only runner and wins that, or at any rate he does well in it—a race to which his peculiarities suit him, or at any rate a race in which they are not a fatal handicap. White's basic fable is the fable of the little misfit who does all right, sort of, and has a life, although it sometimes seems doubtful whether he will. Beneath the humor, it is a wistful story White has to tell.

STUART LITTLE

According to White's own account, *Stuart Little* originated in the late 1920s in a dream he had while on a train trip. "I dreamed of a small character who had the features of a mouse, was nicely dressed, courageous, and questing. When I woke up, being a journalist and thankful for small favors, I made a few notes about this mouse-child—the only fictional figure ever to have honored and disturbed my sleep."[1] White goes on to report that his nieces and nephews—of whom there were 18—would sometimes ask him to tell stories. "In self-protection I decided to arm myself with a yarn or two, and for this I went straight to my dream-mouse. I named him Stuart and wrote a couple of episodes about his life. . . . As the years went by, I added to the tale." In 1930, when he had "perhaps a dozen episodes," he offered them to a publisher, who declined to print them. Seven years later he revised and completed the story. ("I was almost sure I was about to die, my head felt so queer. With death at hand, I cast about to discover what I could do to ease the lot of my poor widow, and again my thoughts strayed to Stuart Little.") He did not die, and Harper's published his book.

Stuart Little began as separate episodes, and the finished work is cheerfully aimless and episodic. It is not until the eighth of the book's 15 chapters that Stuart, and White, come upon the device that will give the story what little central connective plot it has—Stuart's meeting and falling in love with "a pretty little hen-bird, brown, with a streak of yellow on her breast."[2] Her name is Margalo. When, two chapters after she has appeared, she flies away for fear of a cat that is stalking her, Stuart and White have their quest: to search for (but not necessarily to find) Margalo. "While I'm about it, I might as well seek my fortune, too," thinks Stuart (73).

The early, pre-Margalo episodes are all comic turns on what it might mean to be a person with a mouse's size and features, living with a normal family near a pleasant park in New York City. Stuart makes himself useful by rescuing his mother's ring from the bathtub drain, retrieving ping pong balls from tight places, manipulating a hammer that sticks in the piano, and piloting a model ship in Central Park. There are practical problems to solve, big ones for a character of his size and situation: how to wash up in the family's normal-sized bathroom; how to pay the fare on a city bus when a dime is too big for him to carry; how to procure clothes, a bed, ice skates (solution: paper clips). Stuart has misadventures: he gets rolled up in a window shade; he becomes trapped in the refrigerator; he hides from a dog in a garbage can and is dumped onto a garbage scow on the East River.

Nowhere in the first half of *Stuart Little* is it stated or implied that Stuart has a central purpose to accomplish or a primary goal to reach. The general feeling is that Stuart has been born into this wrong-sized world, and his life will be a strange one, hectic in many ways, but with unusual satisfactions in going places where others cannot go. The episodes being stitched together as they are, they make up a sort of free-associational meditation on what it is like not to fit in, to be too small. White's eye is always on the touchingly comic possibilities; he shows no real push for resolution.

Scott Elledge points out that mice turn up with an odd frequency in White's life story, and that White's dream-mouse is peculiarly rooted in White's mind. White's first published poem was about a mouse, Elledge notes; being the youngest and smallest in his family, he may have thought he looked like a mouse. "As a child he kept a pet mouse who was 'friendly and without fear,'" says Elledge. "The first paragraph White ever wrote for 'Notes and Comment' was about buying a mouse trap in Woolworths. And so on" (263).

There may have been particular psychological reasons why White dreamed of a mouse who was "nicely dressed, courageous, and questing," and why that mouse became the hero of his first children's book. On some level White probably identified with Stuart Little and took satisfaction in Stuart's courage as a compensation for his own apprehensiveness. But *Stuart Little* does not seem to be a driven, compulsive book, full of an author's private demons. The story moves good-naturedly around the underlying question, how does one live in the normal world when one is small and odd, and always will be?

The answer to that question, insofar as a slight and playful story like *Stuart Little* can be said to give one, has two parts: first, you do your best to act normal; second, you keep your expectations for success modest and a little vague, and be prepared to live on what the normal would call the margin.

Stuart Little always puts a brave face on things, and he finds that it is not as tough to get by as one might expect. Basically, Stuart proceeds, day to day, as if there were no problem. He sets out to ride a bus, to pilot a model ship, to fill in as a substitute schoolteacher as if there were no doubt that he could do these things. Everybody he meets is remarkably tolerant and even respectful toward him; bus drivers, superintendents, doctors, and dentists all seem to assume that Stuart is all right, nothing to be ridiculed or denigrated. This is a consistent feature of the comedy of the story: Stuart's matter-of-fact manner in absurd situations, situations that he handles pretty well.

But this refusal to grant that there is any insurmountable difficulty in being two inches tall does *not* lead to some simple celebration of the power of positive thinking. The heart of Stuart's problem, it turns out, never was to overcome any sort of prejudice against him. It is to find a purpose for his life. Retrieving rings and ping pong balls, and avoiding the dangers attendant on being the size of a mouse do not (the story suggests) add up to a life. For that, Stuart needs a quest. That is where the search for Margalo comes in.

When he sets out on his quest, Stuart has a couple of small disasters: one when he accidentally starts up an invisible automobile and then cannot stop it until it has wrecked itself; and another when he encounters a girl, named Harriet Ames, who is just his size, makes a date with her, and then builds up his expectations for the date so high that, when things go wrong, his disappointment makes him cancel any hopes for a friendship. He has one triumph, too: he happens upon a school that needs a substitute teacher and spends a brief session instructing the children in what is really important (sunlight, music, the smell of a baby's neck, ice cream with chocolate sauce, and a simple system of law that forbids swiping things and being mean to people). In none of these episodes is the oddness of Stuart's size much of an issue. In fact, in the Harriet Ames episode, it seems as if at last Stuart is the right size for something; but then his own fussiness ruins the prospect. Insofar as one can speak of movement or development in this episodic tale, one can suggest that White's interest shifts away from Stuart's physical peculiarity and turns instead to the oddness of Stuart's attitudes. His stint as a schoolteacher shows that Stuart can dispense with superficial details like roll-taking, arithmetic, spelling and writing lessons, and social studies and get right down to existential basics. His fiasco with Harriet Ames suggests that there is something in Stuart that prevents his accepting ordinary social relationships, even when there are no practical barriers. In a gentle, uninsistent way, White indicates that Stuart has no real home in the world, and that his proper state is to be forever on the road. "I rather expect that from now on I shall be traveling north until the end of my days," says Stuart (129).

Margaret Blount, in her book *Animal Land*, describes Stuart Little's plight as "tragic" and his story as "sad, haunting—some critics have called it sinister"—the "story of an outcast who must always remain so."[3] Stuart is an odd man out, but Blount overstates the pathos in White's story. Stuart is not tragic, because he does not see himself as tragic. He probably knows that he will never fit comfortably into any stable social scheme, but that does not especially bother him. He seems to accept the fact that that is the way he is, and that is the way the world is.

Other reviewers criticized *Stuart Little* for its lack of resolution, and Scott Elledge reports that hundreds of children wrote to White asking him what became of Stuart after he drove off northward in the final chapter. To one of these readers, White "explained" that *Stuart Little* is inconclusive because "life is essentially inconclusive" (Elledge, 260). In terms of the basic fable of White's children's stories, though, perhaps the most appropriate thing to say is that at the end of *Stuart Little*, Stuart seems to be doing pretty well—but doing pretty well at what, one really cannot specify. Traveling north with the possibility of finding his beloved Margalo is not success in any conventional sense of that word, and neither is it really accommodation to the world. But it is apparently purposeful activity that suits Stuart's odd mixture of practicality and romanticism; and, for him, it will apparently do.

WILBUR

Compared with Stuart Little's being a human who looks exactly like a mouse, Wilbur's "difference" in *Charlotte's Web* is distinctly unfanciful and realistic. He is the smallest pig in his litter, a fact that almost costs him his life; and, when he is sold to the Zuckermans, he is the only pig in the barnyard; but there is nothing outlandish about that. Remarkably, though, it is Wilbur, the least bizarre of White's three children's-story heroes, who most explicitly experiences the sense of alienation, of not fitting in and of having no purpose to his life. Of the three, only Wilbur has difficulty finding companionship or a circle of peers. Only of Wilbur is it overtly said, "he wanted love. He wanted a friend—someone who would play with him" (27). Only Wilbur suffers loneliness, boredom, and a feeling of purposelessness. "Less than two months old and I'm [already] tired of living" (13)—only Wilbur says that, though Stuart Little and, later, Louis the voiceless swan have more obvious reasons for feeling a sense of futility. This is one respect in which White's basic fable is more strongly realized in *Charlotte's Web* than in his other two juvenile tales: the main characters most consciously engage its central predicament.

What it takes to cure Wilbur's loneliness and purposelessness, of course, is Charlotte—and the news that the Zuckermans plan to butcher him. That last fact alone is enough to transform Wilbur from saying "I'm tired of living" to shrieking "I don't want to die!" (50). Charlotte's announcing a master plan for saving his life gives Wilbur a reason for living and for caring about what happens. Her becoming his friend makes him less emotionally desperate, and soon the other animals become fairly friendly toward him, too.

Wilbur never really becomes normal in his world, if normality means the pattern that the other characters in the story fit—the farm animals and humans who change, grow up, have mates and children and responsibilities, and die. Wilbur's is an imitation of normality. His big success in life—winning the special prize at the County Fair—rests on the confidence game Charlotte plays on his behalf, so there is the flavor of fakery to it. As for family and social life, he has the succession of spiders who hatch and stay with him each year, serving as surrogate parents, offspring, and peer group for Wilbur. They are not exactly the real thing, but they are close enough. Wilbur's life is close enough to a "natural" one, and it sustains him in a way parallel to the way the quest for Margalo sustains Stuart Little.

LOUIS THE SWAN

The Trumpet of the Swan develops White's basic fable a third time, with some new emphases. Again there is the odd young protagonist, conspicuously unlike those around him, who manages (with a little help from his friends) to shift things and situations around so as to achieve a life that, if it is not exactly normal, provides fulfillment that will suffice.

Communication becomes an issue for the fable and its hero more centrally in *The Trumpet of the Swan* than in either of the earlier stories. All three stories are talking-animal stories, of course, and the rules of communication—who can talk to whom, and how?—are always a question to be settled somehow in talking-animal stories. With White, the rules grow progressively complicated as he moves from book to book.

The Fable

In *Stuart Little,* the situation is pretty simple: all characters—humans and animals—read, write, and speak English and can apparently talk to each other—or write notes, for that matter—if they want to. To be sure, cats and birds never do speak directly to humans in the story; but Stuart converses with them all, and apparently in the same way. Here it seems that animals could talk with humans, and vice versa; it just does not occur to them, or they do not have anything to say to each other.

In *Charlotte's Web* a rule or two has been added. The animals speak English among themselves, and the humans talk to each other. The animals eavesdrop on humans and understand them readily enough; and the occasional human being—Fern, because she is a child—can listen to the animals and understand them. But humans and animals do not talk to each other—whether as a matter of decorum or of practical impossibility is not entirely clear. It is this conspicuous absence of direct communication between animals and humans, as I have noted, that makes the words in Charlotte's web seem miraculous.

Then comes *The Trumpet of the Swan.* For the most part, the principle of *Charlotte's Web* still obtains: swans talk English to each other and people talk English to each other. The swans do not listen to human English much, but they can understand it. (When Louis presents himself to Sam Beaver for the first time, Louis can understand Sam's questions and answer them with nods and shakes of his head.) People cannot understand swan-talk. (When the old cob, Louis's father, goes to pay off his financial debt to the music store, he cannot just tell the store's proprietor what he is there for; Louis has to write a note for him.) Sam Beaver, in some ways a counterpart to Fern Arable in *Charlotte's Web*, is very interested in the whole swan family, but the story never shows him listening in on what they say to each other. "Sam could not make out what the swans were saying; he merely knew they were having a conversation and just hearing them talk stirred his blood."[4]

So, generally, swans speak English to each other and can understand humans but cannot speak directly to them. Humans cannot understand swan-talk (although it is English, which humans can understand when it is written down), but they can speak directly to swans and are only somewhat surprised when the swans can understand them.

And then there is the unique communicative predicament of Louis, the main character. Louis is born, or hatched, mute. To begin with, he (like all swans) can understand everybody, human and swan; but he cannot say anything to anybody. He decides to learn to read and write (he already knows English; he just has to learn the written form). "In that way I will be able to communicate with anybody who can read" (53). He goes to school with Sam Beaver and readily becomes literate; so now he can communicate with people, who can read, but not with swans, who cannot. Then, in order to promote his mating prospects, Louis's father steals him a trumpet, which Louis learns to play. But playing a trumpet is not equivalent to speaking swan-English in this story. The other swans are impressed with Louis's technological approximation of a trumpeter swan's natural call, but he never does succeed in talking directly to them. To the end of the story, Louis can impress everybody, swan and human, with his music; and he can communicate with humans through listening and writing; but he can never communicate in words with his fellow swans. Linguistically, he is more at home in the world of humans than in the world of swans, though ultimately he spends most of his time in the wilderness, away from people.

From this description, it might sound as if *The Trumpet of the Swan* is primarily concerned with Louis's labors to overcome his "speech defect" and to achieve communication. But that is not really what the story is about. White has Louis learn to read and write very readily, and learn to play the trumpet with equal ease. In a few narrative strokes, White establishes Louis in his communicative niche—conversant with humans, impressive to swans—and moves his story on from there. On balance, one would have to say that Louis's primary goal in the story, and White's primary subject, is earning enough money, by playing his trumpet, to pay his father's debt to the music store from which he stole the trumpet.

What appealed to White's imagination in this odd project of a young swan's devoting himself to making restitution for a theft? In his biography of White, Scott Elledge points out a resemblance between

Louis's father in the story and White's own father, Samuel White. In particular, the act of stealing from a music company is significant: in 1899, Samuel White engineered a stock-maneuver with Horace Waters & Co., the piano manufacturing company of which White was general manager and a minority stockholder. By convincing the new and inexperienced president of the company to issue three shares of stock to a longtime cashier of the company, White effectively gained control of a majority of the stock and complete managerial authority. A few years later, the president's wife sued White for fraud. Litigation of the case ran on for six years, and White eventually prevailed; the court held that White's actions may have been unauthorized by the company as a whole, and they may even have been illegal, but they were not per se fraudulent. According to Elledge, Samuel White, generally a conscientious man, "carried a burden of fear and shame" during the years the case was being fought, and after (6).

Sixty-odd years later, that E. B. White should write a children's story in which a character with some his father's mannerisms incurs a debt by stealing from a music store is probably more than a coincidence. Elledge points out, though, that the parallels between Samuel White and the old cob in *The Trumpet of the Swan* are limited. The swan actually steals (Samuel White did not), and he does so because he wants to help his voiceless son (Samuel White's maneuver was made, apparently, because he thought his having control of the company would be good not just for himself but for Horace Waters & Co.; no member of his family had a desperate need like Louis the swan's). There was never any suggestion that White's sons owed anyone money because of their father's action.

In another way, Louis's mission to pay off his father's debts echoes White's own life. A primary motivation for Louis's perfecting his trumpet playing is to make money; likewise, a primary motivation for White's writing *The Trumpet of the Swan* was to make money. As Elledge puts it, "He wrote [*Trumpet*] with the same sense of urgency that twenty-three years earlier had driven him to bring *Stuart Little* to completion—the fear of dying and leaving Katharine inadequately provided for" (345). As White put it, "Like Louis, I needed money" (*Letters*, 644).

The idea that Louis owes a monetary debt is really somewhat arbitrary in the story. Louis seems to be the only one who cares much about it; the music store people obviously do not expect a swan to pay for a stolen trumpet, and White does little in the way of showing that the theft bothers the thief himself, the old cob. But having a debt to pay does create a situation for Louis with which White can apparently identify: he must practice his art not just for itself, or for winning the heart of his beloved, but for money.

The Trumpet of the Swan is the oddest of White's three children's stories, and the least successful with critics and book-buying readers. In a way, its imperfections help to highlight the basic fable of all three.

Although swans in White's story are supposed to be admirable for their simple, natural grace and beauty, the physical image of Louis the swan-hero borders on the grotesque. In full regalia he travels with the following objects hanging from his neck: a slate and chalk-pencil, a trumpet, a money-bag, and a life-saving medal. "I'm beginning to look like a hippie," Louis worries at one point (110). The web of his right foot has been sliced so he can "finger" the trumpet valves. White leaves it to the reader's imagination to work out how a swan's bill could manage to lip a trumpet.

The love story of Louis and Serena is flat and mechanical and not of great interest, apparently, to White; and Louis's quest to make money to pay an ambiguous debt is rather arbitrary and unmotivated. But the very arbitrariness of White's contrivances may indicate, more visibly than the more fluid and graceful *Charlotte's Web* and *Stuart Little* do, what is essential in a White story. At the center is another earnest young character with an inborn difference from those around him—not a pig in an otherwise pigless barnyard this time, or a tiny human who looks like a mouse, but a voiceless swan. He finds, not really a purpose in life, but an odd project that will pass for a purpose. It was strange, but suggestive and poetic, that the mousey human devoted himself to driving forever in search of the little bird he loved. It was implausible, but perhaps not violently so, that the pig's life was saved by words in a spider web that convinced people, irrationally, that the pig was special and should be preserved like a work of art—

and that the pig devoted the rest of his life to befriending generation after generation of spiders. But for a swan to accumulate $4,420.78, in cash, by playing a trumpet for pay is nothing but strange, nothing but a blatant imposition of one kind of "meaning" on a life that would naturally be very different.

More than the other two, *The Trumpet of the Swan* is about the difficulty of easy, natural communication. More than in the other two, White here raises this problem and generates plot with it, and then he resolves it by simply refusing to worry about it any longer: Louis will live a long and happy life among swans, regardless of the fact that he will never be able to talk to them. He keeps alive the memory of his triumphs in the human world by yearly visits to the camp, the zoo, and the Boston Public Garden where he worked as a musician. This, somehow, is enough.

A TWENTIETH-CENTURY FABLE

An obvious question, of course, is why White tells this fable repeatedly in his children's stories. Why or in what sense was it important to him? What did it "mean"?

For one thing, White's is definitely a modern, twentieth-century fable. In its lighthearted, bedtime-story fashion, it concerns alienation, the sense of not belonging, the feeling of oddness in a world where the patterns of normality do not seem perfectly relevant. Chronologically, and in some respects spiritually, E. B. White was of the generation of high modernism that also included T. S. Eliot, Ezra Pound, Ernest Hemingway, F. Scott Fitzgerald, Robert Frost, and William Faulkner. White never would have grouped himself with these authors, would never have called himself a member of any Lost Generation, and had no important dealings, personally or professionally, with its major spokesmen. But there is no avoiding the fact that White's writing, in its less ponderous way, shares in the moods and assumptions that colored "serious" literature in the years between the two world wars.

Eminent among these modern attitudes was a kind of philosophical despair; the feeling that the world of the twentieth century was, spiritually and emotionally, rather a cold place; that Western civilization had been jolted from its foundations by the Great War and the social and political developments that led up to it; that traditional religious and moral certainties had been dissolving for decades, under the critical scrutiny of scientific thinking; that society, its institutions, and its politics, and the philosophical bases for them, were in the process of collapsing. As Bertrand Russell put it[5]:

> That Man is the product of causes which had no prevision of the end they were achieving; that his origin, his growth, his hopes and fears, his loves and his beliefs, are but the outcome of accidental collocations of atoms; that no fire, no heroism, no intensity of thought and feelings, can preserve an individual life beyond the grave; that all the labors of the ages, all the devotion, all the noonday brightness of human genius, are destined to extinction in the vast death of the solar system, and that the whole temple of man's achievement must inevitably be buried beneath the debris of a universe in ruins—all these things, if not quite beyond dispute, are yet so nearly certain, that no philosophy which rejects them can hope to stand.
>   "A Free Man's Worship" in *Mysticism and Logic* (1918)

Or as Joseph Wood Krutch put it: "It is not a changed world but a new one in which man must henceforth live if he lives at all, for all his premises have been destroyed and he must proceed to new conclusions. The values which he thought established have been swept away along with the rules by which he thought they might be attained."[6] Or as Edna St. Vincent Millay put it: "Life must go on; / I forget just why."[7] Like it or not, this was the philosophical landscape in which White had to live.

Modern despair figures in E. B. White's writing not often as a central theme or articulated point of view, but as an emotional ground-tone, a kind of existential melancholy of which his witty commentary is an expression and for which it is a kind of therapy. It would be accurate, wrote White, "to say that there is a deep vein of melancholy running through everyone's life and that the humorist perhaps more sensible of it than some others, compensates for it actively and positively." Humorists (of whom he identifies himself as one) "pour out their sorrows profitably, in a form that is not quite fiction nor quite fact either. Beneath the sparkling surface of these dilemmas flows the strong tide of human woe."

This "woe," in its most generalized form, can be felt behind many of White's satiric comments on "what the world is coming to"—the folly or even madness of modern manufacturing, advertising, government, entertainment, religion, and scientists who "assume that anything is progress just so long as it's never been accomplished before"[8]; it can be felt behind his nostalgia for a simpler, better past; it can be felt in his sentimental affection for children and animals, who are either too wise or too lucky to belong to civilization and its discontents. Occasionally, his mind flirting as fitfully as it did with the realm of cosmic principles, he could imagine the end of the world with a kind of wistful satisfaction. "I think when the end of the world comes the sky will be its old blue self, with white cumulus clouds drifting along," he wrote in an essay for "One Man's Meat." "You will be looking out of a window, say, at a tree; and then after a bit the tree won't be there any more, and the looking won't be there any more, only the window will be there, in memory—the thing through which the looking has been done." And that will be that. "I can see God, walking through the garden and noticing that the world is done for, reach down and pick up and put it on His compost pile. It ought to make a fine ferment" (*OMM*, 294).

A CRUEL EXPERIMENT

White's single most fully developed expression of the modern sense of absurdity and alienation is his short story "The Door" (1939; reprinted in *Second Tree*, 77–82). This takes the form of a stream-of-consciousness report of the thoughts of a man apparently being shown through a futuristic model home, made of strange-sounding substances called "duroid" and "flexsan." The man is thinking about some experiments a professor has done with some rats, training them to expect rewards when they jumped at a card with a circle in the middle, and then driving them insane with frustration by changing the card so that the rats got no reward. Something about the house—the fact that "everything is something it isn't"—makes the man feel like the rats in the experiment, and he starts thinking of his whole life as a similar experiment. "There have been so many doors changed on me." First there was religion—"they would teach you the prayers and the Psalms, and that would be the right door . . . and the long sweet words with the holy sound, and that would be the one to jump at to get where the food was. Then one day you jumped and it didn't give way." The assurances of religion stopped working, "so that all you got was the bump on the nose, and the first bewilderment, the first young bewilderment" (*Second Tree*, 79). There had been other doors he was taught to jump at—including "the door with the picture of the girl on it . . . her arms outstretched in loveliness." But that door, too, was changed. "I am tired of the jumping and I do not know which way to go, Madam, and I am not even sure that I am not tried beyond the endurance of man (rat, if you will) and have taken leave of sanity." Is the madness in the man or in the situation that keeps "changing the doors"?

The fact that White turned to writing for children, and the spirit in which he did it, are on some level related to his form of modern despair. The simple, miniaturized fantasy life of mice, pigs, spiders, swans, and children clearly attracted White as an emotionally preferable alternative to full-blown modern civilization. Even when he permitted himself to indulge in consoling fantasies such as these, however, White carried some of his worrisome preoccupations with him.

White's basic fable tells of a creature with peculiarities who manages, by good luck and some friendly assistance that responds to his yearning, to contrive an odd life that will suffice. This, clearly, is not Eliot's "The Waste Land" writ small, nor Ernest Hemingway's *The Sun Also Rises*, nor Franz Kafka's "The Metamorphosis." Joseph Epstein has gone so far as to liken White to Kafka: "White did develop his books for children in the manner of Kafka, if in a somewhat enfeebled and oddly American way; these books are Kafkaesque but with the

American twist that they are Kafka with happy endings."[9] Here Epstein overstates the case. White was capable of Kafkaesque writing—the story "The Door" demonstrates that. But to find Kafka in *Stuart Little, Charlotte's Web,* and *The Trumpet of the Swan* is to push too hard. White's stories do hint at lostness, alienation, and a basic absurdity of life; but their mood is far from the paranoid nightmares of the tormented Austrian writer.

NEW VS. OLD-FASHIONED

To comprehend the modern quality of White's stories, it helps to contrast them to superficially similar stories from earlier eras. Consider, for example, Dinah Maria Craik's minor classic *The Little Lame Prince* (1875), a sentimental Victorian fable that in some ways parallels White's. Craik's Prince Dolor, like White's heroes, is "different"—he is a lame and sickly child, dispossessed of his throne by a cruel uncle and banished to a prison-tower in the wilderness. Worse than White's Wilbur ever does, Prince Dolor suffers loneliness, boredom, and despair. With the help of a magic godmother who is not entirely unlike Charlotte, the prince learns to venture out with a magic flying cloak and explore the world a little; but, more importantly, he learns to bear his sufferings bravely and to develop patience and endurance from them. The process is arduous, uncertain, and painful; *The Little Lame Prince* is awash with the pathos of his situation. Even his ultimate triumph, when the people of his kingdom come to the lonely tower and by acclamation make him king, is wistful and muted. "When he drove out through the city streets, shouts followed him wherever he went—every countenance brightened as he passed, and his own, perhaps, was the brightest of all. First, because, accepting his affliction as inevitable, he took it patiently; second, because, being a brave man, he bore it bravely, trying to forget himself, and live out of himself, and in and for other people."[10]

He rules his kingdom well. "Thus King Dolor's reign passed year after year, long and prosperous. Whether he was happy—'as happy as a king'—is a question no human being can decide. But I think he was, because he had the power of making everybody about him happy, and did it too; also because he was his godmother's godson, and could shut himself up with her whenever he liked." But it is with visible relief that, at the end of the story, he places his nephew on the throne—"a very fine young fellow; tall and straight as a poplar tree, with a frank, handsome face—a great deal handsomer than the King's some people said"—and flies away to the Beautiful Mountains, which means that he dies and goes to Heaven (*Lame Prince*, 297).

The Little Lame Prince could not have succeeded in the twentieth century, and *Charlotte's Web* could not have succeeded in the nineteenth. The point is certainly not that romantic and Victorian stories are more cheerful or that their endings are "happier." Indeed, Craik sees the matter of *difference*, or being handicapped, as a much more melancholy thing than White does. But she supposes that the wisdom one learns from one's handicaps meshes naturally with public good, and it takes one to Heaven at last. The sorrows of the little prince's life make him compassionate, sensitive, and forgiving, and these qualities make him a good king. Craik's story rests on the assumption that life has more than a private meaning; that goodness is to be realized in society, which recognizes it when it appears; and that to achieve a good life is to have "a kingly nature" with an effect on the world, and worthy of a place in the Beautiful Mountains.

White's Stuart Little discusses, with the children in Miss Gunderson's classroom, what one might do if one were "King of the World"; but the idea is purely fanciful, an interesting question because the possibility of a wise king ruling the world is so far-fetched. Certainly it is unthinkable that Wilbur would become king of the barnyard, or Louis the chief of the swans. In the case of White's twentieth-century seekers, it is enough to find the niche and the project that gets one through the nights and days. A nineteenth-century fabulist like Craik, or John Ruskin, or George MacDonald, or Oscar Wilde, would find White's modest personal aims entirely inadequate. White, on the other hand, would find their visions of transcendent moral and spiritual achievement outlandishly grandiose, so fantastic that they really are not even very appealing as fantasy.

PERSONAL MEANING IN THE FABLE

If White's basic fable shows him to belong to the twentieth century and the generation centered between the two world wars, it also has a personal relevance to the peculiarities of his own life. The fable is, on some level, autobiographical (as earnest fiction almost always is).

There are, of course, obvious ways in which White's juvenile fiction draws on his own experience. Life in New York City as pictured in *Stuart Little*, with its apartment dwellers, doormen, city buses, model boats in Central Park, and garbage scows on the East River, directly reflects White's years living in New York. Barnyard life in *Charlotte's Web* is full of details White observed on his own farm in Maine with its barn and livestock, and some memories of the stable his father kept when White was a boy. *The Trumpet of the Swan* incorporates memories of White's habit, as a boy, of avidly observing birds and other wildlife, and his summers as a counselor at Camp Otter in Ontario as a young man. But by comparison with classics of thoroughgoing autobiographical fiction such as Louisa May Alcott's *Little Women*, Mark Twain's *The Adventures of Tom Sawyer*, and Laura Ingalls Wilder's *Little House* series, White's stories use autobiography in this sense rather casually and sparingly.

It is not on the level of specific facts, settings, and details, but on a deeper imaginative level that White's three stories had the most significant personal resonance for him. The story of the little stranger who achieves at best an irregular "career" and success in life dramatizes something of White's sense of himself.

Here again, it is easy to point out classic children's stories that were tied much more closely to their authors' personal preoccupations than are White's: Hans Christian Andersen writing out his personal yearnings and fantasies in "The Little Mermaid," "The Ugly Duckling," and "The Red Shoes"; Rudyard Kipling dramatizing, in the Mowgli stories, the tensions of an Anglo-Indian boy living between two cultures; or James Barrie in *Peter Pan*, spinning a whimsical myth of mother-love out of his own troubled relationship with his own mother. Compared with stories such as these, so charged with the psychological urgencies of their authors, *Stuart Little*, *Charlotte's Web*, and *The Trumpet of the Swan* are remarkably free and relaxed, and not the work of a man in the grip of unresolved needs and conflicts. Yet the element of personal preoccupation is there at the heart of White's stories.

It may seem odd to think of White as a man who felt he had never really succeeded "in a normal way," when to the outside observer his success was so conspicuous. The humorous and occasional pieces he wrote for the fledgling *New Yorker* magazine, beginning virtually with its founding in 1925, and the essays of his that were sought and printed by magazines and book publishers would seem to be the work of a man who knew exactly who he was and what he wanted to do, and succeeded remarkably.

But the fact remains that intermittently throughout his career White was bothered by the fear that he had not really fulfilled his literary possibilities, and that he had settled for journalism and hackwork that did not entirely express him. In 1933, in a *New Yorker* paragraph, he mused wistfully over his own work. "As the year goes into its dying phase, the thing that most distresses us is the paucity of our literary output. Other than these few rather precise little paragraphs, into which we pour the slow blood of our discontent, we never get around to writing anything at all." He gently scolded himself: "Though we brood a good deal about writing plays and books . . . , a careful search of our premises at the end of a year reveals no trace of a manuscript— merely a few notes on the inside flap of paper-match packs" (*Every Day*, 197–98).

A few years later, in 1937, he began a year's leave of absence from the *New Yorker*, explaining in a letter to his wife: "I am quitting partly because I am not satisfied with the use I am making of my talents, such as they are; partly because I am not having fun working at my job—and am in a rut there; partly because I long to recapture something which everyone loses" when he works creatively against a deadline (*Letters*, 154). During that year's leave, he worked fitfully on a long, pensive autobiographical poem.

Shortly thereafter he contracted with *Harper's Magazine* to contribute a 2,500-word essay once a month, in a department called "One Man's Meat." He produced his essays on schedule, for 55 months; then he resigned. In his letter of resignation to *Harper's* editor Frederick Lewis Allen, White wrote that he was currently "trying to figure out what I had better do about my life, since it is apparent that I am trying to do too many things. I have talked this over with myself, back and forth. . . ." His decision to quit his *Harper's* feature "must seem rather odd and sudden to you, but the truth is I have had great difficulty, all along, writing essays of this sort, as they do not seem to come naturally to me." He confessed to "a peculiar disappointment, almost a defeat, in this. . . . It ought to be the most congenial job in the world for me, and the fault is entirely mine if it isn't" (*Letters*, 238).

8

Conclusion

THE QUEST FOR MEANING

Joseph Epstein sums up this motif in White's life in these words: "He yearned to make something of his life; he yearned to be more than a mere journalist; he yearned—though he never used the word—for significance."[1]

"White was born lucky, as he has often said," writes his biographer, "but he was also born scared" (Elledge, 23). White had, in some respects, a nervous, delicate constitution; he suffered from hypochondria, anxieties, recurrent depression. In 1943 he experienced some sort of emotional collapse, what he called a "nervous crack-up." Sometimes White's apprehensions manifested themselves in his doubts about the value of his writing, his fear that somehow he had never done anything that really mattered.

Probably White's self-doubts were no greater than many people have—especially, perhaps, writers and artists. His "pathology," if one wants to call it that, was mild and intermittent enough that it did not prevent him from achieving a literary career of great eminence.

White wrote each of his three children's stories at a time when it would be understandable that his thoughts might turn to "the meaning of his life." Although composed in parts over a number of years, *Stuart Little* was put into final form, by White's account, during a time of emotional crisis. He had withdrawn from *Harper's* and, with some apprehension, was about to resume editorial duties at the *New Yorker*. He had recently suffered his "nervous crack-up." "I was almost sure I was about to die, my head felt so queer," he wrote in the *New York Times* piece. "With death at hand, I cast about to discover what I could do to ease the lot of my poor widow, and again my thoughts strayed to Stuart Little."

Charlotte's Web was written during an interval of relative tranquility. Once again White had resigned from regular editorial work at the *New Yorker*. Although he continued to contribute to the *New Yorker* on a reduced scale, he had determined to go into a kind of modified retirement on his farm in Maine. "I am starting 1949 in a somewhat relaxed and benign condition as the result of a decision to give up the responsibility of the New Yorker's editorial page," he wrote to his brother Stanley in January 1949. "I intend to apply myself to more irregular and peaceable pursuits for a while, to work patiently instead of rapidly, and to improve the nick of time" (*Letters*, 304–5). Scott Elledge notes that White was 50, "slightly beyond middle age." To White in the 1950s, says Elledge, "the civilized world itself seemed to be past middle age and failing fast. But for White, the most important things that had passed were the sensation and images of infancy, childhood, and youth; and if he could remember them clearly, he could remember the self that had experienced them" (300). White's vision at the time, says Elledge, "was retrospective and his sense of life sharpened by his having seen many things come to an end."

The Trumpet of the Swan came at a more stressful time. Now in his late 60s, his wife suffering from an ailment of the spine and his own health poor, White wrote (says Elledge, 345) "with the same sense of urgency that twenty-three years earlier had driven him to bring *Stuart Little* to completion—the fear of dying and leaving

Katharine inadequately provided for." Of his three children's books, *The Trumpet of the Swan* was the least satisfactory to White; he felt he hurried it too rapidly into print.

Whatever the immediate precipitating conditions, the fact of the matter is that each time White sat down to write a story for children, his imagination turned toward characters who were small and odd, and he contrived successes for them that were balanced precariously on misunderstandings, anomalous arrangements, and rather hazy hopes for the future. It seems fair to say that, in doing this, White told part of the story—not the whole story, but part of it—of how it felt to be E. B. White.

CONCLUSIONS

In the making of stories, there is inspiration, and there is carpentry.

Inspiration works in mysterious, surprising, sometimes brilliant flashes of intuition, insight, visions of heights and depths that seem odd and outlandish; it produces masterpieces like *Alice in Wonderland*, the best of the Grimms' and Hans Christian Andersen's fairy tales, *Peter Pan*, and *Horton Hatches the Egg*. Carpentry works steadily and systematically, following designs and calculations, and produces masterpieces like *Treasure Island*, *Little Women*, the Narnia books, and *The Cat in the Hat*. In works of inspiration, one senses half-understood psychological, philosophical, and even spiritual significance. In works of carpentry, one does not "sense" anything; one sees, and understands, and admires.

In works of inspiration, storytellers seem caught up in ideas or taken over by impulses they probably could not explain if they wanted to. In works of carpentry, storytellers know exactly what they are about, and how and why they are doing it. Works of inspiration tend to break the walls of the familiar and upset things. Works of carpentry provide the house of literature with sound and durable furniture.

E. B. White was a master carpenter, a journalist, a filler of assignments, and a meeter of deadlines. *Charlotte's Web* is a work of first-rate carpentry.

Conclusion

Charlotte's Web was an assignment White gave himself. In 1949, when he began writing it, he was working only part-time for the *New Yorker*; he was looking for an interesting and lucrative writing project; he already had one successful children's story, *Stuart Little*, to his credit. He decided to write a story about animals—specifically, a story about saving a pig.

He had materials that he knew well, and that his readers would know, too, from books, movies, tradition: the old-fashioned farm of a family named Arable ("suitable for cultivation") with a motherly mother, a fatherly father, a rowdy brother in the mold of Mark Twain's Tom Sawyer or Booth Tarkington's Penrod and Sam, a sister who plays with dolls and little animals and who eventually falls in puppy love; a yokel of a hired man named Lurvy; a wise old doctor with a beard; a county fair, a Ferris wheel, a barn with a rope swing, a school bus, sleds, slingshots, bedtime stories and lullabies; a prattling goose and an antisocial rat and a pig that loves slop and mud that is "warm and moist and delightfully sticky and oozy" (11). White's materials were familiar, comfortable, and attractive.

He knew his materials, and he had identified his problem: to come up with an interesting, original device whereby the pig could be saved from butchery. He became interested in "a large spider in the backhouse, and what with one thing and another, the idea came to me" (*Letters*, 375). The spider would be the pig's advertising agent; she would write words in her web that would convince people that the pig was too special to be killed.

White's idea was not inspiration, in the sense I have been using the term, but carpentry, a technical solution to a problem with plot. The spider's web does not become a symbol for something deep or large ("there is no symbolism in *Charlotte's Web*," said White [*Letters*, 614]). Well known and admired as *Charlotte's Web* is, web-writing has not become a proverbial expression of anything. Pinocchio's nose growing when he tells a lie, the "mirror, mirror on the wall" that knows "who's the fairest of them all," the emperor who has nothing on, Peter Pan's flying to the Neverland rather than growing up, even the elephant-bird that comes out of the egg Horton hatches—all these have a proverbial resonance that Charlotte's web does not have. The words in the web do not transform White's barnyard scene; they do not open the door to realms of magic possibilities in the barnyard, because Charlotte is not magic; only the duped human characters in the story are mystified by her. White's traditional barnyard remains the traditional barnyard: the geese continue to lay and hatch eggs; Lurvy continues to slop the pig; children continue to grow up; the seasons continue to change. Charlotte's hoax with her web begins as a solution to a plot question, a trick or a gimmick; and that is what it remains.

The imaginative and emotional magnitude of *Charlotte's Web* is not so much in Charlotte's brilliant idea as in the whole carpentered situation into which that idea fits. Picturing that most hallowed of American settings, the small family farm, White seems to raise the specter of murder in paradise; but then he lays that specter to rest, and he demonstrates in a comforting fantasy that murder will not be permitted, and that the homely farm scene itself contains the agent of love and compassion that will prevent it.

In *The Wind in the Willows*, in a chapter called "The Piper at the Gates of Dawn," Kenneth Grahame tells of a baby otter who has gotten lost; his father and his father's friends fear that the child has been killed. Rat and Mole set out looking for him, and they find him, asleep at the feet of a Pan-like deity, who sings a song:

> Lest limbs be reddened and rent
> I spring the trap that is set;
> As I loose the snare you may glimpse me there
> For surely you shall forget.
> Helper and healer, I cheer
> Small waifs in the woodland wet;
> Strays I find in it, wounds I bind in it
> Bidding them all forget!

Where does this Piper come from? On what authority can Grahame suggest there is a spirit in nature that saves and protects the helpless innocent from harm? It is pure fantasy, a sentimental denial of grim truth, a triumph of wish over reality.

There *ought* to be a Charlotte living in the Zuckermans' barn, even if there is not. The barnyard, as White fondly and nostalgically thinks of it, "having spent so many fine hours there, winter and summer, spring and fall, good times and bad times, with the garrulous geese, the passage of swallows, the nearness of rats, and the sameness of sheep" (*Letters*, 614), should not be the scene of a crime. The pig should be saved ("and I have an idea that deep inside me there was a wish to that effect," said White). The barnyard ought to contain some benign heart, some homely, compassionate creature, even a common spider, who sees to it that murders do not take place.

In the logic of fantasy, what ought to be, is.

A man who on occasions over most of his life felt small and vulnerable, the runt of his litter, sometimes close to death, White could feel for and with Wilbur. A sensitive citizen of the disillusioned twentieth century, he held his fantasy within bounds, not claiming too much: a few friends, safety, security, comfort—that would be enough. A humorist, he kept the mood light with bits of shtick—a rotten egg breaking, a pig trying to spin like a spider, a rat gone obese, a community going nuts over "miraculous" words in a web.

The rest is atmosphere, in White's patented *New Yorker* manner: "this delicious cellar, with the garrulous geese, the changing seasons, the heat of the sun, the passage of swallows, the nearness of rats, the sameness of sheep, the love of spiders, the smell of manure, and the glory of everything."

Appendix
Approaches to Teaching *Charlotte's Web*

White's primary audience in *Charlotte's Web* is children of the ages seven, eight, nine, ten, and perhaps eleven. Probably the ideal way to present the story in the elementary classroom is by reading it aloud a couple of chapters at a time, over several days, at 20 to 30 minutes per installment. The story lends itself well to such treatment, and it breaks into 10 more-or-less discreet units, each with its own kind of completeness or provisional resolution: chapters 1 and 2, in which Fern saves Wilbur from being disposed of and makes him her pet; chapters 3 and 4, in which Wilbur escapes from his pen briefly and then discovers the loneliness and boredom of living in the barn; chapters 5 and 6, in which Charlotte appears for the first time, and the goose hatches her eggs; chapters 7, 8, and 9, in which Wilbur learns that his life is in danger, Charlotte assures him that she will not let him die, spiderwebs are explained, and Fern tells her family about the conversations in the barn; chapters 10 and 11, in which Fern and Avery swing on the rope in the barn, Avery's impulsive attempt to kill Charlotte fails when the rotten goose egg breaks, Charlotte reveals her plan for saving Wilbur, and the words "Some Pig" appear in her web; chapters 12 and 13, in which Charlotte discusses words for her web with the other animals, comes up with "Terrific" and "Radiant" as her next installments, and tells a story about her cousin catching a small fish in her web; chapters 14 and 15, in which Mrs. Arable talks to Dr. Dorian about Fern's preoccupation with the animals, and plans are made for going to the

County Fair; chapters 16, 17, and 18, in which the main characters go to the fair and Charlotte selects her final word for the web; chapters 19 and 20, in which Wilbur wins his special award at the fair and has his "hour of triumph"; and chapters 21 and 22, in which Charlotte dies and Wilbur takes her egg sac back to the barn, where Charlotte's children appear and Wilbur is assured of a lifelong supply of companions.

Charlotte's Web raises a number of issues that children might like to discuss, ranging from the pleasant and comfortable to those that could be sensitive or even painful. Certainly it would be safe, pertinent, and potentially interesting to encourage students to talk or write about their attitudes toward animals, about pets they have had, about the pleasures of keeping animals; about the fun of going to a farm or a fair; about the lives of pigs, spiders, and rats in particular, and perhaps about why those creatures are customarily thought of as disgusting, when E. B. White does not seem to find them so.

Charlotte's Web also takes up the potentially more troublesome subjects of boredom, loneliness, and the need for friends. The story itself treats these subjects optimistically, and leaves no one (not even Templeton) friendless or desperate in the end. Presumably, though, teachers will want to tread lightly in encouraging youngsters to bare their personal feelings about feeling fulfilled or unfulfilled, loved or neglected.

White's story may also arouse thoughts about death—the prospect of one's own death, and the feelings associated with the loss of an older person on whom one depends, such as a parent. Such subjects are extremely delicate, and teachers will probably want to think carefully and cautiously before encouraging young students to talk about them. One can probably compromise by keeping the focus on how White's characters feel, rather than how one feels oneself: What is Charlotte's attitude toward her approaching death? How does Wilbur feel about her dying? In what ways is Charlotte gone at the end of the story? In what ways is she still present? But in approaching such questions, teachers will want to be most discreet; the subject is mined with emotional, psychological, and even religious sensitivities.

Appendix

As the subject of full-scale literary study, *Charlotte's Web* probably belongs more in the college classroom than in junior or senior high school. In general, students in their early or middle teens are not likely to deal well with *Charlotte's Web*. Some may actually still enjoy reading White's story; but they will often feel obliged to take a public pose of superiority to such "kid stuff" and laugh (perhaps defensively) at the idea that a bedtime story is worth their attention. For serious literary study, their time is surely better spent on works that encourage them to "grow up" and that challenge their reading skills, rather than stories that tempt them simply to parade self-congratulatory attitudes toward childhood: works such as *To Kill a Mockingbird, A Separate Peace, The Red Badge of Courage, The Grapes of Wrath*. If for some reason one is committed to "doing children's literature" with high-school students, choose *Watership Down, Kim, Alice in Wonderland*, or some of the harsher Grimms' fairy tales. There is plenty of intellectual challenge in stories like those to keep secondary-school students from feeling that the subject is beneath them.

Most college students are secure enough in their adulthood to approach *Charlotte's Web* as a work of imaginative power and richness in the bedtime-story genre without condescending to it. College instructors may occasionally find students who propose to disallow certain "sophisticated" lines of discussion, on the grounds that the story is for children, and, since children would neither criticize the story analytically nor "find deep meanings" in it, nor consider its relation to other works, literary and otherwise, then neither should adult readers. It is not too difficult to demonstrate the shakiness of that position. *Charlotte's Web*, like any other book, takes its place in the intellectual matrix of whoever reads it; and the notion that, to read it properly, one must pretend to be a child, excluding all knowledge and perceptions unavailable to children, is simply arbitrary, and probably a pretext for just plain laziness.

Charlotte's Web will almost surely be taught and discussed as part of courses in children's literature; it is unlikely to turn up on the reading lists of standard American literature classes, and one does not encounter many seminars on "The Works of E. B. White." It will probably be part of a discussion, then, that involves other talking-animal stories like *The Wind in the Willows, Alice in Wonderland*, Kipling's *Just-So Stories* and Mowgli stories, Beatrix Potter, and various fairy tales. One fruitful approach, then, is to ask just what kind of story *Charlotte's Web* is, within the talking-animal genre. This can begin with basic "ground rule" questions: What, in addition to their ability to talk, seems human about Charlotte, Wilbur, Templeton, and the others? What is stubbornly "animal" about them? Why don't the flies talk, that Charlotte catches in her web? The cocker spaniel that helps to chase Wilbur in chapter 3 does not say anything; why not? Why is Fern so comfortable with the animals' conversing, while her mother is upset by the idea? What attitude toward the possibility of talking animals do other human characters in the story have? In other words, what difference does it make that animals talk in *Charlotte's Web*? To give this question force and direction, one should keep in mind how White's vision of articulate animals compares with Kenneth Grahame's, Beatrix Potter's, Kipling's.

The question of what White does with the talking-animal genre in *Charlotte's Web* leads to other questions. For instructors interested in formal matters of narrative technique, White's story raises some intriguing issues. He begins as if his is to be a story in the realistic mode; in the first two chapters, humans are humans and animals are animals, and no fantasy elements appear. Then we learn that Wilbur can think; then we learn that he and the other animals can speak; ultimately, we learn that some of them can read, and that Charlotte, at least, can write. How does White move the reader along this path of increasing unrealism? Is there ever a point in the story where the reader thinks, "Now that could not happen; that is fantasy"?

Or, in another direction: how serious is White about his humanized animals? Is *Charlotte's Web* an attempt to change people's attitudes toward animals in general—and "disgusting" animals like spiders, rats, and pigs in particular? Does White write like an ecologist, envisioning a democracy of species? Could *Charlotte's Web* legitimately be taken as a fable for vegetarianism? Serious attempts to answer questions like these can make students stretch to articulate their understanding of "how a story means," or what constitutes a responsible, conscientious response to a piece of fiction.

Appendix

As are a great many other children's literary classics, *Charlotte's Web* is on some level about childhood, its rigors and its privileges, and some aspects of maturation. In a spectrum with stories like *Peter Pan* and *The Snow Queen* at one end (with their romantic celebrations of the glories of childhood and the horrors of growing up) and didactic books like *The Adventures of Pinocchio* and *Struwwelpeter* at the other (with their relentless admonitions that children should become disciplined, responsible adults), where does *Charlotte's Web* belong? In what respects is Wilbur a child? Is his innocence and helplessness a moral strength or just a practical weakness? To what extent is his personality based on his potential victimhood? Does he mature over the course of the story, or is he granted eternal childhood? Is childhood here a precious but precarious blessing, as in *Peter Pan*? Is it a failing, a state of moral incompleteness, as in *Pinocchio*? Or is it something else?

On what theory of childhood is Fern imagined in White's story? How does she change, and why? What is one to make of her initial passionate attention to Wilbur, then her becoming a passive observer, and her final losing interest in the barnyard animals? Does Fern "fall from Paradise," as some critics suggest? Is her development a healthy, purposeful maturation, of which the reader should be glad? Does the story of Fern enact the same idea of what it means to be a child as the story of Wilbur does, or a different one?

What type of character is Charlotte? What does she do for Wilbur, and why? Has she more in common with the wise parental figures of realistic fiction—Marmee in *Little Women*, Pa in *Little House on the Prairie*, Badger in *The Wind in the Willows*—or with the mysterious helpers of fairy tales and fantasy—Cinderella's fairy godmother, Rumpelstiltskin (another spinner who saves someone's life), Gandalf in *The Hobbit*, Ruskin's King of the Golden River? Most fundamentally, is Charlotte's role in *Charlotte's Web* in the vein of fantasy or in the vein of realism?

Some learned student may bring up Greek mythology and propose a comparison between Charlotte and Arachne, the Lydian girl who challenges Athena to a weaving contest. Arachne "wins" the contest by weaving an irreverent tapestry showing the gods in their amours, which angers Athena so that she destroys the weaving. Arachne hangs herself, and Athena changes her into a spider, the noose in which she hangs herself becoming a spider's web-line. One could find some slight parallel between the subversive content of Arachne's tapestry and Charlotte's hoax on the human beings, "gods" of the barnyard. It is a very limited parallel, though; there is no Wilbur in the story of Arachne, no altruistic motive corresponding to Charlotte's, no divine retribution. White does not seem to have been thinking of Arachne (nor, for that matter, of those other mythic spinners, the Fates) when he conceived his story.

In a letter to some students in a children's literature class, White wrote offhandedly that *Charlotte's Web* "was a story of friendship, life, death, salvation" (*Letters*, 645). Considerable discussion could be devoted to fleshing out those abstractions, in light of the concrete details of White's story. What is White's attitude toward death here? How exactly are readers supposed to feel about Charlotte's dying? Is it tragic? Naturalistic? Uplifting? Depressing? One might ask students to read White's essay "Death of a Pig" and compare the view of death he presents there with the view implied in *Charlotte's Web*. Does his children's story sanitize, sentimentalize, prettify the subject of death? Or is *Charlotte's Web* the honest and uncompromising treatment of mortality that some of its admirers have said it is?

A discussion of the tone White takes toward Charlotte's death could lead a class into the subtle and challenging task of describing tone in *Charlotte's Web* more comprehensively. Such a discussion could begin simply by asking students to point out passages where certain emotional colorations are obvious. Where does White obviously intend to be funny? Which episodes are conspicuously comic? Is the goose always a comic character? How about Templeton? Is his selfishness funny or evil? How does one know? Is the satiric comedy in the humans' excessive reaction to the words in Charlotte's web similar to the amusement White invites at Avery's violent rambunctiousness, or a different order of thing?

Where, on the other hand, is White sentimental? Which passages seem designed to arouse warm, fond, tender feelings? Charlotte's farewell speech in chapter 21, where she thanks Wilbur for giving her the chance to "lift up my life a trifle"—is that sentimental? How about White's evocation of life in the barn—"this warm delicious cellar, with the garrulous geese, the changing seasons, the heat of the sun, the passage of swallows, the nearness of rats, the sameness of sheep, the love of spiders, the smell of manure, the glory of everything" (183)—is that sentimental? How do the comic and sentimental passages relate to each other? In White, are humor and tenderness compatible feelings, or do they pull in different directions?

Questions like these should be adaptable to various activities in various formats: as foci for journal writing or as material for finished essays; or topics to be discussed by small groups or larger classes. Tactfully pursued, they can enhance an understanding of what *Charlotte's Web* is in itself, and how it figures in the complex web of children's literature generally.

Notes

Chapter 1

1. *Letters of E. B. White*, ed. Dorothy Lobrano Guth (New York: Harper & Row, 1976), 614; hereafter cited in the text as *Letters*.

Chapter 3

1. Eudora Welty, "Life in the Barn Was Very Good," *New York Times Book Review*, 19 October 1952, 49.

2. Pamela Travers, "Tangible Magic," *New York Herald Tribune Book Review*, 16 November 1952, Pt. 2, 1.

3. *Time Magazine*, "The Children's Hour," 8 December 1952, 106.

4. Edward Weeks, "Mr. White's Wonderful Barn," *Atlantic Monthly*, December 1952, 88.

5. August Derleth, Review, *Madison Capitol Times*, 20 December 1952, 16.

6. Scott Elledge, *E. B. White: A Biography* (New York and London: Norton, 1984), 299; hereafter cited in the text as "Elledge."

7. Quoted by Lucy Rollin, "The Reproduction of Mothering in *Charlotte's Web*," *Children's Literature* 18 (1990), 50–52.

8. Quoted by Peter Neumeyer in his essay "E. B. White: Some Aspects of Style." For complete citation for this and the other essays and books mentioned in this chapter, see the Bibliography.

9. Peter Neumeyer, "What Makes a Good Children's Book? The Texture of *Charlotte's Web*," *South Atlantic Bulletin*, May 1979, 66–75.

Chapter 4

1. E. B. White, *Writings from "The New Yorker" 1927–1976*, ed. Rebecca M. Dale (New York: HarperCollins, 1990), 18; hereafter cited in the text as *Writings*.

2. Robert Warshow, "Melancholy to the End," *Partisan Review* 14 (1947), 86.

3. Diana Trilling, Review of *One Man's Meat*, *Nation* 155 (1942), 102.

4. E. B. White, *The Second Tree from the Corner* (New York: Harper & Brothers, 1954), 174; hereafter cited in the text as *Second Tree*.

5. E. B. White, *Charlotte's Web* (New York: Harper & Row, 1952), 85; hereafter cited in the text.

6. *Illustrators of Children's Books: 1957–1966*, compiled by Lee Kingman, Joanne Foster and Ruth Giles Lontoft (Boston: Horn Book, 1968), 193.

Chapter 5

1. E. B. White, *One Man's Meat* (New York and London: Harper & Brothers, 1952), 296; hereafter cited in the text as *OMM*.

2. Pamela Travers, "My Childhood Bends Beside Me," *New Statesman and Nation*, 29 November 1952, 639.

3. "Trade Winds," *Saturday Review of Literature* 35 (July–December 1952), 6; hereafter cited in the text.

4. Joseph Epstein, "E. B. White, Dark and Lite," *Partial Payment: Essays on Writers and Their Lives* (New York and London: Norton, 1989), 318.

Chapter 6

1. E. B. White, "The Librarian Said It Was Bad for Children," *New York Times*, 6 March 1966, 19x.

2. E. B. White, "A Boy I Knew," *Reader's Digest* 36 (June 1940), 35; hereafter cited in the text as "A Boy."

3. Rudyard Kipling, *Just-So Stories for Little Children*, in *Classics of Children's Literature*, ed. John Griffith and Charles Frey (New York: Macmillan, 1981), 881.

4. E. B. White, *Essays of E. B. White* (New York: Harper & Row, 1977), 206; hereafter cited in the text as *Essays*.

5. Henry David Thoreau, "Walking," in *Walden and Other Writings*, ed. Brooks Atkinson (New York: Modern Library, 1937), 601.

6. Kenneth Grahame, *The Wind in the Willows*, in *Classics of Children's Literature*, ed. John Griffith and Charles Frey (New York: Macmillan), 743.

7. E. B. White, *The Points of My Compass* (New York and Evanston, Ill.: Harper & Row, 1962), 63; hereafter cited in the text as *Points*.

8. William Cullen Bryant, "Thanatopsis," in *The Norton Anthology of American Literature*, 3rd ed., ed. Nina Baym et al. (New York and London: W. W. Norton, 1989), 890.

Notes

9. Norton D. Klinghorn, "The Real Miracle of *Charlotte's Web*," *Children's Literature Association Quarterly* 11 (1986), 8.

Chapter 7

1. *New York Times*, 6 March 1966, 19x.

2. E. B. White, *Stuart Little* (New York and London: Harper & Brothers, 1945), 50; hereafter cited in the text.

3. Margaret Blount, *Animal Land: The Creatures of Children's Fiction* (New York: William Morrow, 1975), 244.

4. E. B. White, *The Trumpet of the Swan* (New York: Harper & Row, 1970), 29; hereafter cited in the text.

5. Bertrand Russell, *Mysticism and Logic* (London: Unwin, 1918), 47–48.

6. Joseph Wood Kruth, *The Modern Temper* (New York: Harcourt Brace Jovanovich, 1929), 17.

7. Edna St. Vincent Millay, "Lament," in *The Mentor Book of Major American Poetry*, ed. Oscar Williams and Edwin Honig (New York: New American Library, 1962), 425.

8. E. B. White, *Every Day Is Saturday* (New York and London: Harper & Brothers, 1934), 71; hereafter cited in the text as *Every Day*.

9. Epstein, "E. B. White, Dark and Lite," 318.

10. Dinah Maria Mulock Craik, *The Little Lame Prince*, in *Classics of Children's Literature*, ed. John Griffith and Charles Frey (New York: Macmillan, 1981), 296; hereafter cited in the text as *Lame Prince*.

Chapter 8

1. Epstein, "E. B. White, Dark and Lite," 305–6.

Bibliography

Primary Sources

Books

Is Sex Necessary? Or Why You Feel the Way You Do. By White and James Thurber. New York and London: Harper & Brothers, 1929.

Every Day is Saturday. New York and London: Harper & Brothers, 1934.

Quo Vadimus? Or the Case for the Bicycle. New York and London: Harper & Brothers, 1939.

One Man's Meat. New York and London: Harper & Brothers, 1942.

Stuart Little. New York and London: Harper & Brothers, 1945.

The Wild Flag: Editorials from "The New Yorker" on Federal World Government and Other Matters. Boston: Houghton Mifflin, 1946.

Charlotte's Web. New York: Harper & Brothers, 1952.

The Second Tree from the Corner. New York: Harper & Brothers, 1954.

The Elements of Style. Revision and expansion of handbook by William Strunk, Jr. New York: Macmillan, 1959.

The Points of My Compass: Letters from the East, the West, the North, the South. New York and Evanston, IL: Harper & Row, 1962.

The Trumpet of the Swan. New York: Harper & Row, 1970.

Letters of E. B. White. Edited by Dorothy Lobrano Guth. New York: Harper & Row, 1976.

Essays of E. B. White. New York: Harper & Row, 1977.

Writings from "The New Yorker," 1927–1976. Edited by Rebecca M. Dale. New York: HarperCollins, 1990.

Secondary Sources

Alberghene, Janice M. "Writing in *Charlotte's Web.*" *Children's Literature in Education* 16 (1985): 32-44. Argues that Charlotte is in some ways an ideal teacher of writing, for the effect she has on Wilbur and Fern.

Apseloff, Marilyn. "*Charlotte's Web*: Flaws in the Weaving." *Children's Novels and the Movies.* Edited by Douglas Street, 171–81. New York: Ungar, 1983. Discussion of some ways in which the animated film version alters and weakens White's story.

Elledge, Scott. *E. B. White: A Biography.* New York: Norton, 1984. The definitive biography of White, rich in information and observations placing *Charlotte's Web* in the context of White's life and writing career.

Epstein, Joseph. "E. B. White, Dark & Lite." *In Partial Payment: Essays on Writers and Their Lives,* 295–319. New York and London: Norton, 1989. One of the more skeptical appraisals of White's place in the pantheon of admired writers, this essay surveys his career as a whole and offers some suggestive comments on his children's stories.

Fuller, John Wesley. "Prose Styles in the Essays of E. B. White." Ph. D. dissertation, University of Washington, 1959. Somewhat old-fashioned in its approach, this is nevertheless the most thorough analysis of White's prose style.

Gagnon, Laurence. "Webs of Concern: *The Little Prince* and *Charlotte's Web.*" *Children's Literature* 2 (1973): 61–66. Applies a concept of "living authentically" from philosopher Martin Heidegger to *The Little Prince* and *Charlotte's Web.*

Griffith, John. "*Charlotte's Web*: A Lonely Fantasy of Love." *Children's Literature* 8 (1980): 111–17. Contends that the imaginative heart of White's story is a fantasy of consolation for the fear of loneliness and death.

Howarth, William. "E. B. White at the *New Yorker.*" *Sewanee Review* 93 (1985): 574–83. A concise, appreciative overview of White's literary career.

Kinghorn, Norton D. "The Real Miracle of *Charlotte's Web.*" *Children's Literature Association Quarterly* 11 (1986): 4–9. Among other observations, argues that the world of the barn is a paradise of innocence from which Fern falls, forever lost in the spiritually inferior world of the adults.

Lukens, Rebecca J. *A Critical Handbook of Children's Literature.* Glenview, IL: Scott, Foresman, 1976. Cites *Charlotte's Web* for examples of various fictional techniques: plot, style, character development.

Mason, Bobbie Ann. "Profile: The Elements of E. B. White's Style."

Bibliography

Language Arts 56 (1979): 692–96. Stresses the clearheaded, economical, unsentimental directness of White's writing, in *Charlotte's Web* and elsewhere.

Neumeyer, Peter F. "The Creation of *Charlotte's Web*: From Drafts to Book." *Horn Book* 58 (1982): 489–97, 617–25. A detailed examination of White's drafts, partial drafts, and notes for *Charlotte's Web*. Focuses particularly on White's difficulty in arriving at a satisfactory beginning for his book and the comparatively late addition of Fern Arable to the story of Charlotte and Wilbur.

——. "E. B. White: Aspects of Style." *Horn Book* 63 (1987): 586–91. Identifies certain techniques of repetition, juxtaposition, and variation of stylistic levels in White's prose, drawing examples from his children's stories.

——. "What Makes a Good Children's Book? The Texture of *Charlotte's Web*." *South Atlantic Bulletin* May 1979: 66–75. A suggestive, though perhaps overreaching article that finds classical, epical, and archetypal qualities and connotations in White's story.

Nodelman, Perry. "Text as Teacher: The Beginning of *Charlotte's Web*." *Children's Literature* 13 (1985): 109–27. Drawing on several narrative theoreticians and psychologists, Nodelman argues that the two realistic chapters, which begin *Charlotte's Web,* serve to educate the reader in how to read the rest of the story; the opening chapters tell in "naive" or "innocent" terms the same story of a pig's rescue as the chapters about Charlotte and Wilbur tell in a more sophisticated way.

Rollin, Lucy. "The Reproduction of Mothering in *Charlotte's Web*." *Children's Literature* 18 (1990): 42–52. A sophisticated Freudian commentary on how "mothering" operates with Fern, Charlotte, and Wilbur.

Sale, Roger. *Fairy Tales and After: From Snow White to E. B. White.* Cambridge, MA: Harvard University Press, 1978. A free-ranging, somewhat impressionistic discussion of what *Charlotte's Web* says and does; offers a number of insights into the story and White's achievement as a story-maker.

Sampson, Edward. *E. B. White.* New York: Twayne, 1974. Surveys White's literary career through the early 1970s; remarks on *Charlotte's Web* particularly emphasize Fern's role in the story.

Solheim, Helene. "Magic in the Web: Time, Pigs, and E. B. White." *South Atlantic Quarterly* 80 (1981): 391–405. Presenting itself as "a kind of preface" to White's work, this essay touches discursively rather than exhaustively on a number of aspects of White's writing, giving most attention to a philosophically suggestive "web-image" Solheim finds recurrent in White's work.

Stahl, J. D. "Satire and Evolution of Perspective in Children's Literature: Mark Twain, E. B. White and Louise Fitzhugh." *Children's Literary Association Quarterly* 15 (1990): 120–21. Briefly traces the emergence of "a satiric voice" in children's literature, with attention to *Charlotte's Web*.

Index

Index

About the Author

John Griffith is Associate Professor of English at the University of Washington. He is co-editor, with Charles Frey, of the anthology *Classics of Children's Literature* (New York: Macmillan, 3rd. ed., 1992) and co-author, with Charles Frey, of *The Literary Heritage of Childhood* (New York, Westport, CT, and London: Greenwood Press, 1987). He has published scholarly articles on a variety of American authors.